I Met God
in Bermuda

Faith in the Twenty-First Century

First published by O Books, 2009
O Books is an imprint of John Hunt Publishing Ltd., The Bothy, Deershot Lodge, Park Lane, Ropley,
Hants, SO24 0BE, UK
office1@o-books.net
www.o-books.net

Distribution in:	South Africa
	Alternative Books
UK and Europe	altbook@peterhyde.co.za
Orca Book Services	Tel: 021 555 4027 Fax: 021 447 1430
orders@orcabookservices.co.uk	
Tel: 01202 665432 Fax: 01202 666219	Text copyright Steven G. Ogden 2008
Int. code (44)	
	Design: Stuart Davies
USA and Canada	
NBN	ISBN: 978 1 84694 204 4
custserv@nbnbooks.com	
Tel: 1 800 462 6420 Fax: 1 800 338 4550	All rights reserved. Except for brief quotations
	in critical articles or reviews, no part of this
Australia and New Zealand	book may be reproduced in any manner without
Brumby Books	prior written permission from the publishers.
sales@brumbybooks.com.au	
Tel: 61 3 9761 5535 Fax: 61 3 9761 7095	The rights of Steven G. Ogden as author have
	been asserted in accordance with the
Far East (offices in Singapore, Thailand,	Copyright, Designs and Patents Act 1988.
Hong Kong, Taiwan)	
Pansing Distribution Pte Ltd	
kemal@pansing.com	A CIP catalogue record for this book is available
Tel: 65 6319 9939 Fax: 65 6462 5761	from the British Library.

Printed by Digital Book Print

I Met God
in Bermuda

Faith in the Twenty-First Century

Steven G. Ogden

BOOKS

Winchester, UK
Washington, USA

CONTENTS

ACKNOWLEDGEMENTS

I want to thank the reading group of Stephen Hayter, Robert Martin, Oleg Morozow, Bill Nicholls, Gloria Parker, Lee Parker, Tim Sarah, Baden Teague and Kathy Teague. Over red wine and camembert, we met to road-test the book and entered into robust discussion about life, death and faith. Thanks to Christine Beal for proofreading and Stephen Downs and Lee Parker who went the extra mile, providing much needed wisdom. A special thanks to my parents Geoffrey and Nellie, who taught me a lot about the meaning of integrity (I'm still learning).

Lastly, I am indebted to my wife Anne as her goodwill and generosity of spirit have helped me realize another project.

Steven G. Ogden

PREFACE

Apparently, Christianity has passed its use-by date. It is out of favor with the urban, time-pressed, latte-sipping, wine-quaffing, emailing postmodern West. From London to New York, the Church, the Bible, God and Jesus are cause for embarrassment, even hostility. After all, who wants to be known as religious? I accept the contentious nature of religion. Consequently, I focus on the problem of God and argue that God is a problem because God is absent, especially in the experience of suffering. And because the old man in the sky has let us down, the key question is where on earth is God?

The assumption here is that faith is not undying belief in a dreary set of timeless propositions. On the contrary, faith is a dynamic attitude to life. So, we need to begin with human experience. While experience is not everything, it is an important starting point. At the least, we have access to our experience. In particular, our experience forces us to face the reality of the absence of God and the experience of absence forces us to rethink God.

I am not attempting to write a proof of God's existence, but I am undertaking an exercise in redescribing God. I accept as a given that our experience is messy. Yes, ambiguity is evident in the mundane tasks, moral dilemmas and complex relationships of everyday life. I assume that there are no simple answers. Nevertheless, a new description of God can enrich and inspire human life and community by using the idea of absence. Above all else, there are fleeting but exquisite moments of the presence of God in the world.

CHAPTER 1

THE KISS OF DEATH

Life is messy and we are constantly tidying it up, though a few of us have given in and refuse to use our mobile telephones or return emails and of course, we never, never file. In spite of this, many people are searching for a life-giving, life-grounding faith, which makes some sense of the ambiguity of life.

Once upon a time religion, in particular Christianity was regarded as the repository of faith. However, for many reasons, Christianity is now widely regarded as irrelevant, embarrassing or offensive. This is largely because of its failure to address the problem of suffering, that is, how can a good God let bad things happen?

An Occupational Hazard

My wife calls me *the kiss of death*. This term of endearment came out of our experience of attending numerous wedding receptions. As a priest, I have the opportunity of participating in many of these festive events.

Typically, as we enter the reception, the first thing we do is look at the display board, which reveals the incomprehensible mystery of the seating arrangements. We are usually placed on table number 17, the so-called miscellaneous table. The table is positioned toward the back of the reception room, next to the table where the three-piece wedding band adjourns for a beer, a bowl of fries and a large plate of stale, white-bread chicken sandwiches. But now the fun begins.

On such exalted occasions, I wear a clerical or dog-collar with my dinner suit. This means that as we meander across the room toward our table, the guests freeze with dread, suspecting that the priest is coming to sit at their table. As we pass by successive tables, their sense of relief is palpable and in some cases audible as guests can be heard to mutter, what sounds like an expletive but could be mistaken for a prayer, "Thank God! He's not sitting here."

Eventually, we arrive at Table 17.

Our table party consists of Uncle Bob (a retired engineer who attends all family weddings and funerals), Trevor the trusted family accountant, Shona the bride's long-lost girlfriend from high school, and a shy, anonymous cousin from Manchester. They are polite but uncomfortable, though they try in vain to mask their obvious misfortune. As we sit down, they all sit up straight, bolt-upright. Their ashen faces cry out "no drinking, no swearing, no dirty jokes and no fun".

In due course, they all relax as we share in the good natured table banter and indulge in a couple of glasses of red wine. Without fail, the guests proceed in turn to announce emphatically "I am not religious" or "I'm spiritual, but I don't go to Church". With all and sundry having nailed their colors to the mast, we end up having a wonderful evening full of animated conversations about families and work, success and failure, life and death and our shared search for meaning. What I find fascinating is that they do not see these big-life issues as coming under the radar of religion.

Regrettably, the evening draws to a close. After the formalities have concluded and the newlyweds have departed, it is time to say goodbye to our table companions. Shona, the bride's long-lost girlfriend, who has been freely drinking expensive champagne all evening, gives me a half nelson hug and thanks me passionately for listening to her life story. One by one the remaining table companions say in all sincerity that they enjoyed our company and they were surprised to discover that we were normal. Sadly, all this leaves us with mixed feelings.

On the one hand, clergy are widely regarded as objects of ridicule, even contempt, because religion for many people is an embarrassing phenomenon. God is a problem in general in Western culture and whatever you do, please do not mention Jesus. Accordingly, the so-called endearment *the kiss of death* is a form of gallows humor. Sure we had some laughs, but the wedding experience reminds us that my presence, and what I represent, is a source of consternation. On the other hand, I appreciate the disquiet surrounding religious institutions and their representatives, and I suspect the other guests at Table 17 were responding to a bad experience or a damning image of what I call bad religion. As a result, I am claiming that there is something important; let's call it good religion, which gets lost in the institutions, hierarchies, formalities and dogmas of the Church.

The starting point to resolving the problem is the way we think and feel about God, but why is God a problem in the first place? The God problem is basically a credibility problem, which in part has to do with the failure of the Church to practice what it preaches. In the main, it stems from the experience of suffering. In the midst of suffering, where is God? Indubitably, God's absence is conspicuous. My paternal grandfather died when I was nine years old. I did not attend the funeral, which was not unusual then, but I recall with remarkable clarity my parents returning from the funeral, as they had purchased for me a fine looking book as a means of solace. I cannot remember the gifts they brought back for my siblings, but we all got something. My book was about farm animals and it had big, bold, colored templates. As I thumbed through the pages of that beautiful book, I felt overwhelming sadness. What struck me then and still affects me now was a rogue thought, seemingly from nowhere saying "so much for God". I was bitterly disappointed with God. God's silence was deafening.

In my young mind, God had promised much, but had failed to deliver. This God is the absent God. It was a painful realization, because this was precisely the time I expected God to come good. I felt sad about the loss of Pop and greatly disappointed because the old man in the sky had let me down. Thus, the term *the kiss of death* has a number of levels of meaning. On the surface, it's a story about a wedding reception, which provides a simple measure of the clergy's standing in the wider community. Beneath the surface, it expresses a profound sense of collective disappointment. God and the Church promised to deliver so much, but failed on the most important life-question, the question of suffering. Further, the ultimate experience of suffering is death, the death of a dream, a lover, a child, a parent, a friend and the death of hope itself.

It is in the face of death that we feel the absence of God most keenly. I suspect that the public perception of the Church's response to suffering then is a reliable barometer of how people judge the value of clergy, Church and God.

The history of suffering represents a judgment on God. Consequently, God has failed. In short, this is *the* God-problem. If you like, suffering is the litmus test of religion and while the God-problem is broader than the question of suffering, the reality of suffering raises the problem most acutely. So, it is hard to know what to make of God in the twenty-first century. Unsurprisingly, the God problem is also a stumbling block for those who want to believe. Now there are many possible responses to the problem, ranging from denying that there is a problem in the first place to abandoning God altogether. In my case, I want to wrestle with the problem.

It is partly an intellectual endeavor, but there are personal reasons too. As a human being, I want the life of faith and the experience of living in a faith community, but not at the expense of sacrificing intellectual and personal integrity. In the main, however, I cannot believe, endorse or promote the traditional or dominant Western understanding of God without making major qualifications. For instance, while I enjoy using many, but not all, of the traditional images and metaphors of God in public worship and personal meditation, they are nonetheless images and metaphors. In themselves, they do not constitute God. Nevertheless, while many practicing Christians do not believe that God is an old man with a long beard sitting on a throne in the sky, there is a substantial cultural legacy in the West of a God who is just like this, who intervenes in history, fixes personal problems and resolves moral dilemmas in the twinkling of an eye. In reality, it is hard to get this idea of God out of our heads. This view of God, who looks like Charlton Heston's portrayal of Moses in *The Ten Commandments* or the caricature of God in *Monty Python and the Holy Grail*, prevents many Christians from thriving and discourages others, who would thrive in a faith community, from approaching the Church's doors. All said, this old man in the sky, this king, this judge, this holy warrior and cosmic ruler, is the God who has failed us abysmally on the question of suffering.

I am responding to a complex and highly charged problem. As such, I am not intending to be prescriptive, because the issues of God and the Church in Western culture are multifaceted. Certainly, the issue of how God, Jesus, the Church and Christianity relate to our contemporary world is thorny, vexing and loaded with all sorts of historical and cultural baggage.

Moreover, one of the Church's many credibility problems derives in part from the claim that it has *the* answer. On that note, let me reassure you from the outset that I do not conclude this book with anything like "that's why Jesus loves you" or "purchase my book and the DVD and you will be saved (or your money back)". There are no short, pithy answers to universal questions about climate change, world peace, the quest for meaning or rising interest rates. The promise of a succinct conclusion runs counter to the sheer density of real world issues. However, I am hoping to encourage exploration of faith, in particular, of faith in God for the real world. In the real world, there is a myriad of issues ranging from war, racism, poverty, hunger, disease, drug addiction, cloning, the exploitation of women and children, to divorce, blended families and loneliness. Of course, many voices are trying to be heard as they seek to address these mind-numbing, heart-breaking issues. In this context, an immediate and eminently practical question is where does the Church fit into this complex global conversation?

While I will not be exploring the nature and purpose of the Church, something needs to be said about it now, so as to remove potential distractions that may prevent us from rethinking and re-experiencing God. I do not want the Church, or our preconceptions of the Church, getting in the way of our exploration. Personally, some of the richest experiences of my life have been in churches that have bravely tackled the big issues of life at great personal cost. All the same, many people like the guests at Table 17 see the Church as completely irrelevant. Further, the word *church* itself conjures up images of old stone buildings, empty and musty, controlled by eccentric and insensitive clerics who resemble the self-important parsons of Jane Austen novels. The clear and somewhat painful impression is that the Church is not at all related to twenty-first century concerns. In other words, the life and significance of the Church does not touch the real world. The inference is often drawn that thinking people do not attend church or believe in God. There are exceptions, such as members of the chattering-classes who attend church on the sly for aesthetic and cultural reasons (aaah! a robed-choir singing Mozart). Naturally, they do not believe in God. Some, of course, hide behind the veil of an ill-conceived agnosticism, but most of these thinking-people cry vociferously "I am not religious".

In the meantime, the mainstream Church remains silent as Christian fundamentalists, who dominate our tabloid papers and television sets, have something shrill to say about everything. Fundamentalism has become so vocal, strident and brazen, that it is often seen by the wider public as speaking for all Christians.

Unfortunately, there is no clear distinction in the popular mind between mainstream and fundamentalist Christianity.

In conclusion, the present era, our era, is a God-wrestling era. However, I believe that by engaging with the big issues of the twenty-first century and suspending certain traditional beliefs, it is possible to use the word *God* meaningfully and to affirm that there is an intimate relationship between God and the world. This God will not be the same as the Sunday school God with whom many of us grew up. Like a heavenly puppeteer, the Sunday school God works over and above the world, pulling the strings and manipulating earthbound marionettes. While this description of God is in no way intended to offend thousands of Sunday school teachers, it is recognition that an adult person needs to develop an adult view of faith.

The Church also needs to outgrow outdated views of God and make room for alternative views. In short, the image of a Sunday school God is a metaphor for what is known as *theism* (see Chapter 2). Subsequently, I am setting out on a journey, a faith journey, in which I ask why the Church is wedded to a theistic view of God. What if, instead of the traditional view that God is an external creator who intervenes from the outside, God is found in the real world in the complex network of relationships (human, ecological, cosmological), and maybe, just maybe, in our shared human experience?

The God Problem

In exploring this alternative view of God, a number of assumptions are made. I recognize the intellectual and social problems associated with using the word *God* in contemporary Western culture, and that's partly why wedding guests at Table 17 proclaim, "I am not religious". The word *God* calls to mind countless unflattering, and disdainful images like religious zealots, fruitcakes, do-gooders, God-botherers, bible-bashers, televangelists and fundamentalists of all persuasions. Where does this reaction come from? At 3am on Australian television, on any given day, there is usually at least one televangelist on air, in full flight, called something like Leroy van Bank. Typically, the way Leroy speaks about Jesus, God and the Devil is truly cringeworthy. He believes that the mythological figure of the Devil *actually* exists and his audience squeals with delight every time the Devil's name is mentioned. The audience's response to the Devil's name is like children at a pantomime, who greet the arrival of the mustachioed villain with rapture, as his sinister presence heightens the dramatic tension. In both situations, Leroy's and the pantomime, the tension seems more satisfying than the promise of its resolution. However, in Leroy's situation, there is every chance that vulnerable people are being disturbed and manipulated by this perverse form of hero-worship, which finds its focus in the enduring fascination with Leroy and the Devil (followed by Jesus and God in that order).

In terms of my concerns, the problem is the prevalence in tabloids and on television of the fire and brimstone anti-heroes of the religious right, who give the false impression that all Christians are like this. For instance, eminent biologist Richard Dawkins uses Leroy-like images to represent and condemn mainstream Christianity when he writes statements like, "the interventionist, miracle-wreaking, thought-reading, sin-punishing, prayer-answering God of the Bible".

In terms of baggage, another issue needs to be named. In the last decade or so, a number of clergy in the US, Australia, Europe and elsewhere have been convicted for offences relating to child abuse. While the majority of clergy are innocent of such appalling acts, we were all part of an inward-looking culture that fooled ourselves into believing that acts like these could never happen in the Church. There is a theological dimension here too, which propagates an idealized view of the Church and the Christian family. The idealized view is misleading, dishonest and dangerous. It is the kind of view that presumes God is in heaven and all is well, so consequently, we do not need to exercise wisdom and discernment in either our faith communities or our families. We are Christian and evidently Christian families are perfect families.

This toxic combination of a heavenly God, removed from earthly realities, with a naive and over-confident Church proved diabolical. There is no doubt that a certain way of idealizing God, clergy and Christian families helped to create this dangerous in-house culture as we did not feel obliged to take the normal precautions or set the standards, which were observed in society at large.

In short, this is just some of the contemporary baggage that comes with the word *God*. In an honest and transparent approach to today's big issues, these negative associations need to be named, as the process of naming may help some people discover that there is a life-affirming alternative to Leroy van Bank's life-denying pathology. However, while mainstream Christianity is radically different from Christian fundamentalism, there is a certain view of God, which they hold in common. This is the God of extreme or hard theism, the old man in the sky.

The God of hard theism is rightly linked to the Crusades, anti-Semitism, witch hunts, the Inquisition, racism and sexism. This is not to say that God or religion or individual Christians single-handedly caused these events. These events have many interrelated causes. However, the God of hard theism lends itself to human attempts to control and exclude others. This is the God who rules, judges, punishes, saves and intervenes in world events at will. I call this *the Car Park God*. I have heard people say that they prayed to God, as they were racing to get to a meeting, and God got them a car park. While this type of prayer surfaces mainly in fundamentalist circles, for many of us there is the temptation to resort to the Car Park God under duress (as in the evening before an examination).

However, there is a profound issue at stake here and this is the

9

failure of *this* God to intervene successfully for millions of innocent people. Where was the Car Park God at Auschwitz? This failure is a constant source of sadness, anger, bewilderment, disillusionment and cynicism for the inestimable casualties of human history. It raises *the* theological question of our day: *Where is God?* Where is God in the earthquakes, floods, fires, famines and plagues of history? Where is God in the sacking of Constantinople in 1204 (when Christians slaughtered Christians)? Where is God in the Holocaust? Where is God in September 11, Iraq, the Sudan or Zimbabwe? However, before we can even begin to approach these hard questions, there are a number of preliminary problems that need to be raised.

The first problem could be glibly described as a public relations exercise, but it is ultimately about relevance. The second and related problem has to do with re-interpreting the meaning of God and Jesus, which is my main focus. The first problem has to do with the fact that many people outside the Church think Christians worship something like *the old man in the sky*. For many practicing Christians, the experience of suffering has brought about a radical rethinking and re-casting of God. We no longer worship *this* God. But this is not the impression the wider community has of the Church. This is partly due to the Church's retention of ancient language and rituals, so that while the meaning of its symbols has changed, the archaic forms have remained the same. From the outside, this is confusing. Personally, I find the experience of the shared meal of bread and wine a life-giving experience (also referred to as Holy Communion, Eucharist or the Mass). From the outside, it may seem a quaint, meaningless, even ghoulish ritual, especially if it is assumed it is done for the benefit of soothing a cartoon-like wrathful God. This has not been helped by the fact that some churches are not good at the kind of hospitality that fosters understanding, participation and inclusion.

The impression that Christians are appeasing a punitive God is reinforced by the tendency of leading Christian fundamentalists to monopolize the media limelight. This is compounded by the media's fascination with the absurd, eccentric and offensive actions and pronouncements of fundamentalists. Consequently, it is hard for people not to associate the word *God* with such baggage. It is like a psychologist saying to her students, "Don't think about camels". Naturally, we cannot get those darn camels out of our heads. Likewise, whenever God is mentioned, we cannot get *the old man with the beard on a throne in the sky* out of our heads. The second problem relates to the on-going task of re-thinking and re-describing God, Jesus and the Church. There is a risk here. What if God cannot be re-claimed? Nonetheless, I work on the assumption that faith is renewed by taking a risk and addressing rather than suppressing questions and that the process of addressing questions is a profound expression of faith itself.

The current invitation to explore, to make the journey, is not an excuse for shoddy thinking or sloppy writing; as I will try to explain and justify claims clearly and fairly. The exploratory nature of the work itself reflects something of the search for faith. It presumes that if Christianity is going to be relevant in the twenty-first century, then it has to address the big issues of the day, seriously and adequately. It has to be accountable. The big issues in the real world demand this kind of accountability. I distance myself completely from any form of fundamentalism. Nonetheless, the meaning of the term *fundamentalism* is hard to define in strict terms. Suffice to say, fundamentalism here refers to religious fundamentalism in general, and Christian fundamentalism in particular. There are considerable differences between Christian fundamentalism and mainstream Christianity. Naming and addressing these differences may help some people find or reclaim another view of God and even experience good religion.

Fundamentalism zealously believes it is the exclusive keeper of the truth. While some traditionalists in the mainstream Church may share this view, the majority of the mainstream holds the truth more lightly and generously, that is, that there is room for doubt and respect for a range of views.

Typically, Christian fundamentalism expresses its cherished truths in moral or theological absolutes, that is, its rules apply everywhere and in every instance, and it supplements, supports and articulates these truths by using ancient (pre-modern) stories, as proof texts demonstrating the faultlessness of their position (such as the assertion that homosexuality is wrong and the Bible unequivocally supports this position). Fundamentalism accepts mythological or legendary stories as factual (Noah's ark). The Bible then is life's instruction manual, from which particular insights can be immediately gleaned and applied, regardless of time, place and circumstance. Ironically, fundamentalists are not consistent in their application of a literal interpretation and this gets them into hot water, but they are consistent in seeing the Bible as inerrant. The Bible is true regardless of any gaps, discrepancies or contradictions. Thus, fundamentalists possess the truth. They own it, lock, stock and barrel.

In contrast, in the mainstream Church there is wide acknowledgment of the symbolic or existential value of these stories, as well as recognition that ancient stories need to be re-interpreted for today's situation. Further, fundamentalism, using militaristic language and images, believes it has been divinely authorized to invade and colonize mainstream Christianity as well as other religions and philosophies, because it owns the truth. This God, and the kind of religion it spawns, leaves me cold. It is barely Christian. Consequently, I assert that an alternative understanding of God needs to be articulated for the sake of the wider Church and for those who are seeking a relevant expression of faith. .

Possibilities

The epithet *the kiss of death* is a reminder of the negative, even ludicrous view of God that is widespread in our time. We need an alternative description. A twenty-first century God is not found in the sky but in the network of relationships and the idea of a network of relationships can provide a new way for talking about faith. Further, an account of the human condition that does not address the issue of the absence of God in suffering is at best trivial and at worst meaningless. This interest in the absence of God is more than a passing academic fad, because suffering is universal; crossing cultural and religious divides. Above all, most of us have known the pain and the betrayal of God's absence. Subsequently, absence raises a major issue for the Church and its relationship to the wider community.

How can we speak with credibility about God in the world, if we ignore God's absence? Either we concede God is *absent* in every sense of the word or wrestle openly and audaciously with our concept of God, until it accounts for the ambiguity of experience. Now, historically, there have been numerous God-wrestling eras and this is one of them. Curiously, God-wrestling in the twenty-first century is characterized best by a sense of ambivalence. On one hand, God is absent and that is the end of the matter and on the other hand, the idea of God is being re-visited with enthusiasm and is providing new insights from a variety of perspectives. In the twenty-first century, there are many ways of re-describing God. This is a good thing, so long as re-descriptions consider the issue of suffering.

On that basis, new descriptions of God, new models, new metaphors and new symbols, will need to canvass the absence as well as presence of God. Significantly, this represents a radical shift in understanding faith because, as well as our stereotypes about God, many of us grew up seeing faith as steadfast belief in a predetermined set of timeless propositions. This is an unrefined, static and fragile view of faith. I am advocating a view of faith that is dynamic and robust, which is conceived in terms of shared human experience.

As children, many of us made *houses* from playing cards, patiently and meticulously, card by card we built these fantastic fragile structures. There was no glue holding the cards together, as they rested perilously against each other on edge. However, a breeze, a bump or the removal of a card, especially from the base, and the house collapsed. Likewise, a faith that is constructed on the basis of a disparate collection of propositions, superficially linked by buzz-words or word-association is doomed to collapse. Therefore, I am extending an invitation to go on a journey, which entails leaving behind the idea of God as an old man in the sky and the misconception of faith as belief in a set of propositions, which falls like a house of cards when it comes under intellectual scrutiny and the reality of suffering.

For the investigation to proceed, I am recommending the suspension of particular traditional Christian beliefs and preconceptions. Now the idea of the suspension of beliefs is not the same as denial or rejection. Moreover, I am arguing that this process of suspension is an inherent feature of the life of faith. It recognizes the transitory nature of human language, concepts and rituals.

Further, traditional beliefs are suspended because they represent a form of *in-house* language, which is largely indecipherable to the wider community. Generally, the Church's doctrinal statements and theological symbols ring true for practicing Christians in religious settings, that is, they make sense for Christians in the life of a particular faith community.

In contrast, I am oriented towards the world as well as the Church. I am trying to look both ways and wrestle with what it means to be a person of faith in the twenty-first century. Therefore, no religious statement, symbol, story or figure is exempt from scrutiny, especially the figure of Jesus. Think for a moment about how loaded the name of *Jesus* is in the twenty-first century. For example, at your next dinner party, as the soufflé is being served, try saying "I'd like to talk about Jesus". Although Jesus is the central figure in Christianity, and there are good reasons for starting with him, a lot of religious and cultural baggage needs to be found and ejected if Jesus is not to remain an unqualified source of embarrassment.

CHAPTER 2

THE GRAND TOUR

I am not wedded to the old theistic God of mainstream Christianity. This is the God of hard theism. Vestiges of this God remain in the mainstream Church, obstructing spiritual growth and enshrining institutional structures. The twenty-first century needs an alternative portrait of God. Therefore, I am presenting the basis for a redescription of God, that is, an alternative way of thinking and feeling about God (a new theology). I am trying to find a way to redescribe God, which is not set in concrete by the ritual, polity and dogma of the Church or captive to the made-to-order spirituality of the contemporary world. I will use a number of tools and guides to assist us in this enterprise. To that end, I am relying on sound argument, the motif of the journey, the disciplines of history and philosophy as well as the work of two German scholars (our German shepherds, Tillich and Rahner).

The Grand Tour

The development of a faith fit for the twenty-first century demands that we embark on a journey, in order that we will be challenged and shaped by the new. My wife Anne and I made our first serious journey in 2007. We were away for five weeks and we stayed in Hong Kong, London, Bermuda, New York and San Francisco. Subsequently, our Grand Tour provides the book with a simple framework for dealing with complex matters. By framework, I mean a series of images or backdrops, which like the ancient slideshow or the contemporary PowerPoint presentation invites reflection.

I am using the journey motif for three reasons. First of all, we had a wonderful time (and none of our friends want to see the 1,231 photographs). Second, we had to go on a journey and leave some things behind in order to be open to, and opened by, new insights. We were innocents abroad, such that many things had an element of surprise, catching us off guard, challenging us to think and feel differently. Third, there is something about a journey, and the motif of journey, which is timeless and universal. In particular, the idea of a renewing and redefining experience lies at the heart of the religious pilgrimage. Today, the idea and phenomenon of *the tourist* dominates the world stage. Commercial interests and cultural impact aside, the idea of tourism taps into this primal interest in the journey.

Lastly, I am inviting two German scholars, Paul Tillich (1886-1965) and Karl Rahner (1904-1984) to join us as travelling companions. They will be used to help us reconsider the figure of Jesus and the meaning of the death and resurrection, which is the acid test of the credibility of Christianity.

The true measure of the greatness of a scholar is that his or her work is impossible to read or understand, that is, if it takes three hours to read a page, then it is evidently profound. Clearly, this is not always the case. While the works of Tillich and of Rahner are difficult to follow, they produced great insights. If you want to explore them further, I suggest you first look at Tillich's sermons and radio broadcasts and Rahner's sermons and prayers. However, for the purpose of my argument, you do not need to know much about them at all. I am also calling them our two German shepherds. The metaphor of a German shepherd conjures up images of guide and protector. Now, we once owned a beautiful German shepherd called Jack. Jack was completely useless as a guard dog, but he was great company. In the past, Tillich and Rahner have offered guidance, but above all they have proven to be reliable companions for those who are willing to take risks. In that sense, they will be our shepherds, our companions on the way.

On a practical note, while there is a series of excursions (or excurses) throughout the book, it is designed to be read without their assistance. These excursions provide supplementary background information on key issues. They are optional extras. In addition, I use a few insights from history and philosophy to further understanding. Nonetheless, I will keep technical jargon to a minimum and when new terms are introduced, they will be explained. I am also using pairs of concepts to make significant comparisons and to provide useful insights (*good/bad* religion, *hard/soft* theism, *fundamentalist/mainstream* Christianity). While there are differences between each member of a pair, which mask variations and exceptions, these comparisons enable us to see familiar things with new eyes. For example, the use of the pair *good religion* and *bad religion* challenges the endemic presumption that all religion is inherently bad or that good religion is flawless or monochrome.

Now, I will be the first to draw attention to bad religion. The fact that I know Christianity from the inside, despite some of my own blind spots, means I can analyze it on the basis of experience rather than hearsay evidence. In contrast, on the basis of experience, good religion can create and sustain human community.

I am not trying to make universal truth claims for all people, places and cultures. I am writing primarily for a twenty-first century Western culture. I am trying to speak to those people, inside and outside the Church, who are looking for a twenty-first century faith. I am not intending to say that the Western context is a clearly defined entity or that it is superior to other cultures or settings. It's the one I know. From my experience, the idea of Western culture conjures up images of figures like Shakespeare, Bach, Newton, Descartes, Napoleon, Dickens, Darwin, Queen Victoria, Freud, Picasso, Pavarotti, Madonna, Tiger, Hillary and

Obama and places like America, Australia, Canada, New Zealand, the United Kingdom and Europe. However, as soon as you make a list you offend some group because you left it out. Moreover, on the surface, mistrust of the institutional Church seems more prevalent in Western Europe and Australasia than America. However, there are American academic circles that equally share this mistrust and contempt of religion, who would also think of me as *the kiss of death*. Today, the lines of demarcation are becoming blurred. For example, fundamentalism has historically been influential in America, but now fundamentalist groups are growing in number and influence in Australia. Thus, *the West* represents a cluster of overlapping histories, sub-cultures, lifestyles and values.

The main role of history is putting people, events and ideas into context, so that they can be better understood. That is, sometimes we do not understand the significance of historical figures or events until we have an idea of the setting. Once a figure or event is put in context, we often say, "Now I get it". However, history alone does not solve all the problems. There are religious issues that the discipline of history cannot adequately address, without the aid of other perspectives. Moreover, the discipline of history has its own problems. For example, there is wide recognition of the problems associated with the selection and interpretation of historical facts. In particular, it is not always easy to identify a fact clearly (why did Napoleon lose the battle of Waterloo in 25 words or less?). Facts do not speak for themselves and someone has to interpret them. The task of interpretation is also more complicated than simply listing facts. However, I do not intend to go to the other extreme of arguing that facts are not important or unattainable. Therefore, it is important to clarify the limits of history.

For instance, there are a number of books around today about Jesus, with many claiming to have found new and decisive facts about him that are irrefutable. Mmmm. Historians make judgments about *facts*. Nevertheless, they often disagree, that is, they provide different interpretations of the same facts (as an example, note the different views on the impact of European settlement on indigenous Australians). So, facts are not listed arbitrarily. They are sorted, ranked, grouped, embellished or understated on the basis of the historian's judgment and bias. Certainly, the gathering and reporting of facts is essential, but the impact of the historian is equally important. The historian is part of history and so it is important to understand aspects of an historian's (or a philosopher's or a theologian's) social and historical context.

I use philosophy in two ways: to develop a concept of experience that has credibility and to explain key concepts. So a brief discussion about philosophy will highlight some of the problems it holds in common with other disciplines and reinforce the need for the use of complementary approaches.

In broad terms, philosophy is about thinking rationally in a methodical way about the world, belief and the conduct of life. Like other scholars, philosophers work in collaboration and competition with peers in an attempt to establish their arguments. Traditionally, philosophy has been regarded as different from other disciplines because the object of its thinking is thinking itself. In some ways, it has seen itself as a little superior. In terms of its own history, the application of philosophical thinking led to the emergence of the Enlightenment of the eighteenth century. During this period, the influence of the Church decreased, while correspondingly, confidence in scientific achievements, human reason and progress increased. Philosophy helped foster the Enlightenment's confidence in reason and thus, who needs God when you can use your mind? This contributed, directly and indirectly, to the marginalization of the Church.

The Present Era
I am interested in finding new ways of talking about God in the

world. This is a large territory to cover, so it is important to make some additional qualifications. First, I am writing for the twenty-first century Western world. It is not the same world that my grandfather knew. I doubt whether he ever saw a computer or knew what one was. It is a postmodern world. So let me illustrate what I mean by postmodern. I have already indicated that one way to kill off a dinner party is to mention the name Jesus. However, if you simply wish to annoy your hosts by showing up their ignorance, then slip a reference to postmodern into the conversation as the canapés are being served. Something like, "Oh darling, that vase with its lack of symmetry and clashing colors is *so* postmodern". The word *postmodern* is a buzz-word for the new, especially the new that breaks with the old conventions. It can be used as either a compliment or an insult, often both at the same time. Historically, it has been linked with art, architecture, literature and philosophy. I am using it as a broad way of describing the era and the world we live in, that is our twenty-first century world.

In short, postmodernity represents the next historical period following modernity. This helps in identifying the issues we have to face, which previous generations did not have to address. Therefore, I will provide a working definition of the term *postmodern*, which signals changes in our world and our thinking, including changes relating to the meaning and place of religion. Undoubtedly, we see ourselves and the world differently from earlier generations; especially in the way we interpret what it means to be human and the nature of experience. A typical *postmodern* view is that there are many ways of seeing the world and no one view is absolutely right. It is a kind of organized chaos that questions the conventional wisdom of the past in relation to politics, history, philosophy and theology.

Further, the absence of God is a feature of modernity. This is because modernity focused its attention on the material world to the exclusion of the spiritual. It is based on what Charles Taylor describes as "closed world structures" in which there is no place for the transcendent. Further, the material world, which is regarded as objective, is invested with positive moral value. It's real. It's factual. It's true. It's a good thing. It's a moral benefit. In contrast, the spiritual world, which is regarded as subjective, is invested with negative moral value. It's not real. It's not factual. It's a dubious thing. It's a moral deficit. Therefore, the gap between the material and the spiritual is a standard feature of modernity and this, combined with a new understanding of how things are caused, led to the situation where modernity implies the absence of God. God does not fit in. The divine does not register. Therefore, if the term secularization means the decline of religion in the West, then the absence of God can be described as a symptom of secularization. Not everyone agrees with this view. What is more, the meaning of *secularization* is arguably less clear in postmodernity. In modernity, there was no place for religion at all. In postmodernity, it's okay to talk about religion (at least in some circles). For example, New Age gurus have apparently discovered *true religion* or a *new personal spirituality* that is infinitely superior to the *old institutional religion*.

Excursion, Secularization: Sociologist Peter Berger challenges the idea that we live in a secularized world. In an early work, Berger refers to the secularization process in terms of "the alleged demise of the supernatural". More recently, he describes the thinking behind secularization as an unproven theory. He claims that the relationship between modernity and religion is more complex than simply an either/or scenario (though he does not offer a solution). For him, it is a difficult task to define secularization, let alone assess the extent to which secularization has occurred. It is an equally difficult task to compare religions in terms of their relationship to modernity. Further, Berger claims that while interest in mainstream Christianity appears to have waned in Europe (falling church attendance); there has been growth in other areas (Islam, fundamentalist Christianity). He argues that the situation in Europe has not been satisfactorily researched and that interest in religion may have become diffused rather than diminished. For him, the changes in Europe reflect "a shift in the institutional location of religion". Others, likewise, contend that secularization is not the disappearance of religion but its differentiation and consolidation.

In conclusion, these discussions on supposed *trends* do not address the main issues. Hypothetically, if *no one* believes in God, this does not necessarily mean God is absent. Conversely, if *everyone* believes in God, this does not necessarily mean God is present. Incidentally, Berger suspects that secularization theory is a product of "a globalized *elite* culture". However, I suspect there are many groups in Western society who think the influence of religion has waned, not only academic *elites*, but sections of the media and the chattering classes.

I am using the term *postmodernity* as a tool, in the sense of a syndrome, where a syndrome is a cluster of recurring symptoms or features (like religious pluralism). There are also historical grounds that support the idea of postmodernity as a new and distinctive historical period. For instance, Hans Kung sees the end of modernity and the beginning of postmodernity as occurring between 1918 (loss of life, new treaties, new borders) and 1945 (Holocaust, Hiroshima). The two World Wars played a major role in changing lives, nations and ideas and influenced a growing mood of disenchantment with modernity's faith in human reason and progress. Postmodernity proper, however, emerges as a distinct period during the 1960s. The sixties witnessed the beginnings of major social, political and cultural transformations in Western culture. A series of historical developments took place that changed Western thinking, ranging from the Bay of Pigs (1961), the assassinations of John F. Kennedy (1963) and Martin

Luther King (1968) to Vatican II (1962-5), Beatle mania and the rise of pop culture (1963-7), birth control, the sexual revolution and the landing on the moon. Moreover, the Tet offensive (1968) disturbed American and Western self-confidence and led eventually to the Paris Peace accords (1973). There was a parallel upheaval in theological and ecclesial circles with the advent of *Death of God* theology, which harks back to a media event in 1966 in the *New York Times* and *Time* magazine. In 1968, Pope Paul VIs encyclical (*Humanae Vitae*), which reaffirmed the censure of artificial contraception for Catholics, undermined the authority of the Church and its leaders in the eyes of many Catholics and interested onlookers. Since the sixties, social and political changes have taken place almost exponentially. The dismantling of the Berlin Wall (1989) and the apartheid system in South Africa (1991) represent major political and social changes. There have been ground-breaking developments in cosmology, genetics, reproductive medicine and computer technology.

In brief, postmodernity is a new period in history, that is, it is the period that follows modernity. There are significant differences between the two periods, which become more pronounced over time. There are other factors too, relating to religious pluralism, new understandings of language and the human person, which underline the distinction between the periods of modernity and postmodernity. In particular, the new understanding of the human person and community and the notion of human experience as shared experience is of great importance in my re-description of God.

Pluralism is a feature of postmodernity. Basically, the concept of pluralism means that there are different ways of experiencing, seeing and describing the world in which we live. Different groups, cultures and religions understand life and the meaning of life in different ways. The interest here is primarily in *religious* pluralism. Religious pluralism is not new, but what is new is a keen sense of awareness about the ethical, philosophical and

25

cultural implications of these differences. For instance, pluralism challenges the view that there is only one legitimate God, sacred book or code of moral conduct. Part of this new awareness involves the value judgment that all religions are of equal value or are worthy of equal respect and that no one religion can lay claim to possessing a privileged position on matters of truth and knowledge. In religious pluralism, no religion is superior to any other. Naturally, this is vehemently disputed by fundamentalists who think we are all doomed to drown in the treacherous sea of relativity.

Religions have traditionally presented their claims to uniqueness or superiority in the form of an all-defining master-narrative. This is *the big life story* which makes and shapes a religion. It could be described as a meta-narrative, grand-narrative, even mother-of-all-narratives, but the term *master* with its nuance of *control* better suits its historic character. The master-narrative functions like a template that is superimposed over individuals, communities and cultures. It has the effect of homogenizing local social, ethical and religious traits. For example, the nineteenth century Christian missionary movement, in Africa and elsewhere, worked with a one-size-fits-all European model of Christianity. In this classic instance, and others like it, religion can induce conformity through the power of its master-narrative, which legitimizes the superior status claims of the religion by declaring that it is *the* fount of all wisdom. Pluralism, however, challenges the traditional Christian claim to uniqueness and superiority. It makes us all wary of setting Western views of God in concrete, as if we possessed *the* master-narrative.

New interest in the nature of language is also a feature of postmodernity. This interest has its predecessors. The philosopher Wittgenstein turned his attention to language as it was used in everyday activities: "the meaning of a word is its use in the language", this means that we work out the meaning of a word on the basis of how it is used in everyday speech. This gave rise to his notion of the language game, that is, a language has to be inter-preted on the basis of how it is used. For example, the meaning of the English word *God* does not fall from the heavens as a discrete linguistic unit with an obvious, unequivocal meaning. Consequently, there is a new respect for the way words work together in various combinations, in diverse settings, to give rise to new meanings. It is no longer entirely clear how a word relates to the object it is meant to represent. For example, what logical reasons are there for saying that the word *rose* stands for a particular flower? Moreover, if we accept the word *God*, what does it represent and how does it achieve this?

The issue of language is related to pluralism. For example, an individual learns a religion like learning a language, that is, by participating in it. Therefore, the challenge in postmodernity is to speak meaningfully about God, because the meaning of a word is found *in* the use of words and not *behind* them. As one scholar puts it, it is not the case that the truth is "out there". We have to remember too, that we have inherited ancient language and theological assumptions about the meaning of God, which are in part captive to the social milieus they evolved in, and yet permeate and influence language today.

A new development in the idea of *person as subject* is also a feature of postmodernity. Here is a simple illustration. A child develops his/her identity not in isolation, but in relation to others. (I recall from my feeble attempt at Psychology 101, something about rats going berserk, if they are not properly socialized). A child, given genetic and environmental parameters, learns who he/she is by interacting with parents, siblings, aunts, uncles, teachers, playmates and maybe even the Sunday school teacher. The point is that we are not of our own making, since we live in the world and interact with the world.

It may seem strange, but it is only in comparatively recent times that we have thought of ourselves as either a thinking-self or conscious-subject. Initially Descartes, building on the legacy of people like William of Ockham and Martin Luther, took the idea of a person as subject to a new level. In Descartes, the person as subject was an abstract, atomized concept, "But what then am I? A thing which thinks. What is a thing which thinks?" In everyday life, we have a primal sense of *ourselves* as *selves*. For example, as I am writing this sentence, I am aware that I am writing and wondering what you are making of it. What is more, while you are reading it, you are aware that you are reading it and that I am drawing your attention to your capacity for self-awareness. In practice, we have a sense of ourselves. While the nature of the meaning of self or subject is hotly debated in philosophy, theology, psychology and the cognitive-sciences, there is growing recognition that we are not formed in isolation. We know intuitively from experience, unless we are dreadfully deceived, that our sense of self evolves in relation to others and the world around us. In musical terms, we learn to sing in concert with other voices. Just as we influence others, others provide the descant for our chorus.

In postmodernity, we are not islands; we are inter-dependent persons. Our identity is not plucked from nowhere, but discerned in an evolving network of relationships. This is the idea behind the buzz-word *intersubjectivity*. This is a formal way of referring to the fact that we find out who we are in relation to others and the world. All this reflects a gradual movement away from an atomistic to a holistic understanding of humankind. What it means to be a person is discovered on the basis of our network of relationships, that is, human subjectivity is *inter*-subjectivity. Our formation as a person takes place in concert with others; even our response to experiences in solitude is partly pre-conditioned by the impact of others on our personal formation. While the idea of intersubjectivity does not explain everything, it is a useful term that recognizes the ongoing role played by social interaction and cultural factors in the formation of human identity and community. It is partly the basis for my understanding of the naturę and significance of human experience, which becomes the context for redescribing God. For our purposes, intersubjectivity is the setting for interpreting the experience of God as presence and absence, where experience, and that includes religious experience, is shared, mutual or corporate experience, which is formed and sustained in relation to others and the world.

I am arguing that Christianity is out of favor with our urban, time-pressed, let's-do-lunch, wine-quaffing, emailing world. I accept as a given the troublesome nature of religion. In particular, I am asserting that God is a problem because God is absent, conspicuously so in the experience of suffering. In contrast, an authentic re-description of God has to incorporate the reality of God's absence. In fact, the experience of absence forces us to rethink God. I also accept as a given that human experience is ambiguous and this is evident in the complexity of everyday life, but I argue that a re-description of God can enrich human life and community. All this is oriented toward and set in a postmodern context. *Postmodernity* is a fashionable term, which turns some people off because it is the latest thing. Technically, it is used to cover many themes in architecture, art, literature, philosophy, theology and the social sciences. For me, postmodernity stands for a new period in history. This is our era, the postmodern era, and this is the context for making new discoveries. While there is no clear boundary between postmodernity and modernity, there are substantial differences between the two periods. These differences are based on historical factors and the following three characteristics: pluralism, language and intersubjectivity. Furthermore, history is not neat, but I am using a simple time-line in order to place ideas, events and people in historical context:

Pre-modern: before the seventeenth/eighteenth centuries

Modern: from the seventeenth/eighteenth centuries to the middle of the twentieth century

Postmodern: from the middle of the twentieth century to today

Excursion, Modernity and Postmodernity: The emergence of modernity as an historic period has links with the marginalization of the Church, because in modernity, God is irrelevant or absent. The word *modernity* comes from the Latin *modernus*, from the adverb *modo* (equivalent to *nunc* meaning *now*). It involves judgments about the past in the light of the *now*. These judgments involve a distancing from the past, because the past is regarded as outdated. The past is *passé*. It is no longer *in* or *fashionable*, because the new has become the rule by which we judge the worth of everything. While the roots of modernity are found in the thirteenth century; modernity proper emerges with the eighteenth century. Ideas and events associated with modernity include reason, progress, tolerance, secularization, individualism, nationalism, urbanization, industrialization and land consolidation.

In modernity, sharp distinctions are made between the material and the spiritual, the objective and the subjective, the external and internal worlds. A materialistic world-view emerges in which positive value is ascribed to the human capacity to interpret phenomena in mathematical-like computations. Reason is prized because it enables individuals to think and act *correctly*. Consequently, a person is considered primarily as rational, and the spiritual dimension is relegated or dismissed, because it is not regarded as rational or sensible. Inevitably, the Church becomes redundant as God is declared unnecessary and/or absent.

Postmodernity poses its own challenges for religion.

As William Hamilton expresses it, in postmodernity there is "No unmoved mover, no gods, no prophetic longing for righteousness, no Jesus restlessly healing and teaching and running risks". There are many possible responses to these challenges. Some scholars see postmodernity as an opportunity to overcome modernity's shortcomings, rather than as a problem to be solved. Others refute the existence of postmodernity as a distinct historical period. Others recognize the challenges of postmodernity, but they do not see it as a distinct historical period. In all these, postmodernity as a distinct historical period is downplayed or discredited. Admittedly, it is difficult to establish postmodernity as a distinct historical period in unequivocal terms.

CHAPTER 3

THE CONGESTION ZONE

Experience is crucial, but what do we mean by it and when we talk about experience, what happens to issues concerning truth? Real life is chaotic and experience is ambiguous and amorphous. The Church has sanitized experience, making it harder to discover and articulate a twenty-first century faith. In particular, the mainstream Church has perpetuated an idealized view of life, family and relationships, which gets in the way of faith. For most of us, life, family and relationships are wondrous, woolly and worrisome. Subsequently, this chapter looks at how the Church has sanitized experience, the complex nature of experience and the issue of truth. In the process, fundamentalism is used as a contrast to show what I mean by truth. The result is a modest view of truth as new wisdom that emerges from our mutual experience.

A Sanitized View of Experience

There are many good reasons for testing our ideas about God. The issue of suffering is central. Specifically, the experience of the absence of God is conspicuous in human suffering. When the chips are down, where is God? It is this experience of absence that forces us to rethink and redescribe God. Clearly, this is not a trivial matter or an academic exercise. We cannot glibly dismiss doubts and questions about God, because many of us have experienced first hand the disappointment and pain of the absence of God. However, for the sake of clarity and understanding, what do we mean by the idea of *experience*?

In practice, we continually experience ourselves, others and the world. We are familiar with the *reality* and importance of our own experience, whether it takes place in solitude or in community. We recognize that there are times and places where experiences are life-defining in terms of personal and corporate history and identity.

As an illustration, "Are you experienced?" is the name of a Jimi Hendrix song. I have a copy of it in a cardboard box full of diaries, photographs and vinyl LPs. In the late 1960s, I became enthralled with the music of the iconic guitarist Hendrix. I remember the day he died. I was 15 years of age. In his honor, and to the disquiet of our teachers, we made a small funeral pyre in the middle of the school cricket pitch. Naturally, we were showing-off, but I recall a sense of loss. I cannot remember expressing this aloud to my friends, but we knew in an instinctive, rough-edged way that we had experienced a sense of loss and that this was a shared experience. It did not matter that none of us knew Hendrix personally.

What mattered was that we sensed, to our surprise, that deeper things had been stirred. It is like watching a play: we know it is *out there*, but somehow it gets *inside*. Like good ritual, it ferments powerful emotions. In this case, it was grief and as with all grief, other losses came to the surface. It was a powerful experience.

Historically, the Church has had a mixed attitude to experience. On the one hand, there has been an unrelenting focus on sin as a feature of human existence. On the other, when the Church has explored other more positive dimensions of experience, its idealistic distortion of Christian faith, life and family has unwittingly become an obstacle to faith. First of all, sin as a measure and symptom of human frailty, has been given a lot of air-time in prayers, hymns and sermons. In that context, sin is usually addressed in a serious and solemn manner. In recent years, a more positive view of the inherent value of humankind and human experience has emerged across the mainstream

Christian traditions. In keeping with these developments, the focus has shifted from remnants of pre-modern magical-thinking (about church, sacraments and doctrine) to the importance of Church as a people-in-community, within which the symbolic significance of ritual and doctrine come to life. In fundamentalist churches, however, sin is habitually addressed in a punitive manner, emphasizing Christians as people who perceive themselves to be dreadful sinners and who love to sing, pray and talk about sin incessantly. This is partly because fundamentalism is pathologically locked into pairing God as a good creator and supreme judge with humankind as an innately evil and dependent creature. In reality, take away fundamentalism's pessimistic view of existence and you take away its life-force.

In contrast, and to the credit of mainstream churches, there has always been an emphasis on the gratuitous and inclusive love of God, which is manifested as grace. However, the term *grace* is a sickly-sweet concept when it is removed from real life and sanitized for the sake of pious consumption in the context of the myth of the perfect life.

Second, for centuries there has been a comparatively negative view of family within the Church, because a monastic, single and celibate view of human life was held up as the ideal. Eventually, the focus shifted to the family. Since the Victorian era, the Church has openly and consistently sanitized human experience by means of the myth of the perfect family. In particular, the Church has been captive to projecting and maintaining idealized views of the life of faith and the so-called *Christian family* (with the associated catch phrase *family values* which has entered political campaigns). But what exactly is a *Christian* family? Surely, its not just happily married heterosexual couples with children? What about unhappily married couples? What about single parent families? What about married couples who no longer have children, cannot have children or decide not to have children? What about single and divorced people, gay and lesbian couples and single people? And what about the extraordinary incidence of domestic violence and sexual abuse in so-called ordinary families?

In reality, the idealized view of the family is burdensome for many people who feel excluded by the narrow definition and maudlin associations of the *Christian* family or who are crushed by the sheer weight of circumstance, failure or tragedy. Unsurprisingly, this idealized view is a barrier for those seeking the life of a faith community. In many a Mother's Day worship service, all and sundry wax lyrical about the debt of gratitude we owe our saintly mothers, who single-handedly created our perfect families. But what if your family life is somewhat screwy? What if your mother is drunken, cruel or neglectful? What if you desperately want to be a mother, but are unable to conceive? As a consequence, the *average* attendee leaves the church crestfallen, thinking "I'm just not good enough" because he/she does not measure up to these impossible standards.

Mainstream Christianity's sponsorship of the myth of the perfect life can be just as debilitating as fundamentalism's obsession with sin, the Devil and the wrath of God, because the idealized view of life, faith and family is a denial of the ambiguous nature of experience. It represents a refusal to acknowledge the reality of the absence of God. In marked contrast, the experience of absence is an indispensable ingredient in what makes a real life and an authentic faith and as such it calls into question the way we think and feel about God, faith and family. In all honesty, we either concede that God is *absent* in every sense or we wrestle honestly and passionately with God, until our understanding of God (our theology) makes a modicum of sense of the ambiguity of human experience. As a result, I am arguing that, in protest against the suffocating effect of the promotion of the so-called Christian family, experience is messy.

In the twenty-first century, the failure to adequately address the question of absence has led to the Church losing trustworthiness. Trust and goodwill are hard earned and even harder to regain once lost. Subsequently, the Church and its God have become marginalized in the West.

The marginalization began in the late Middle Ages, accelerated under the influence of various philosophers and developed during the Enlightenment of the eighteenth century in tandem with the emergence of the modern era. Its finale occurred in the nineteenth century, with the philosopher Nietzsche pronouncing the death of God. In our era, the nature of God's marginalization has changed. In modernity, God was displaced from the world. In postmodernity, God is displaced, but there are other gods with their own claims on truth (religious pluralism).

In modernity, the divide between the material and spiritual was a defining feature. In postmodernity, there are two major streams. Some argue that there is no spiritual or religious dimension, partly because there are so many religions, as if to say, "Who can you trust?" So religion is discarded as being a purely psychological phenomenon, possibly a by-product of the evolutionary process. Others argue that, while we can reclaim the spiritual dimension, no single religious tradition can own or control it because there is no master-narrative. The irony with postmodernity is that, while challenging sundry claims to religious superiority, it gives permission to discuss issues concerning religion, spirituality and values.

So what does this all say about experience? The Church has tended to promote the myth of the perfect life and in so doing it has sanitized and homogenized experience. Subsequently, to break the shackles, we need new metaphors. Where do we begin, as there are many possible ways of redescribing human existence?

Here's one, which harks back to the Grand Tour. As we travelled, our eyes were opened to new ways of seeing the world. In that context, London's congestion zone is an apt metaphor for human experience. The zone is a designated area in central

London in which a charge is applied to motorists, apparently with the aim of reducing the use of private cars in the zone. I am not sure if the scheme works but, whether on foot or by car, our stress levels rose as we entered the congestion zone. While it was stressful, it was also very exciting for this couple from the Antipodes. It brought home, that life is not neat and the lack of neatness does not necessarily detract from the richness of experience. The rules or regulations we make can improve or enhance life, but they do not iron out the wrinkles. In fact, the wrinkles give life its richness and its diversity. For many in the West, we live permanently in a congestion zone. There is no exit. Most people I know are worried about their work, their relationships and their sanity. People in general worry about responsibilities and deadlines, health and security, happiness and death, as we all try to distil some kind of meaning from life's successes and failures, achievements and mistakes, joys and sorrows. Yes, the congestion zone is a better metaphor at capturing life's complexities than the Church's apple-pie view of the world.

On the basis of sermons and public announcements from church leaders, it is easy to gain the impression that church life consists largely of beautiful hymns, harmonious congregations and perfect families. This is the stuff of myth, the myth of the perfect life, which sanitizes experience and estranges people from faith and each other. The myth is supported by an unshakeable confidence in an omnipotent and omnipresent God. This is the God of hard theism. Consequently, there is no room here for doubt about bedrock matters. The classic example of this is the long history of insufferable sermons routinely preached on Mothers' Day. Many a Christmas sermon too, addressing weighty matters of peace and poverty, has been performed with an over-confidence in God that belies the fragility and ambiguity of the human predicament. Unfortunately I have preached a few of those cheery Christmas sermons, and so I am conscious of the seductive power of the idealized view of self and family, faith and

God (and public speaking). The challenge is to address the issues of suffering, the absence of God and the meaning of faith. In terms of experience, real experience, Good Friday and the meaning of the Cross resonates more deeply and truly for many Christians than any other sacred day. On that day, suffering is named and the absence of God is acknowledged. This view of Good Friday, however, is not to be confused with the fundamentalist feeding frenzy over *the blood of the Lamb* liberally shed to appease a wrathful God.

Experience

For many people, childhood experience of the Church was deadening (at best tedious, at worst punitive) and as a result many have been inoculated from an early age against discovering an adult view of religion in general and Christianity in particular. Religion is deadening when it does not resonate with experience, that is, our personal experience, our collective experience and our historical experience. So, religion that does not consider experience is bad religion.

The word *experience* is part and parcel of how we describe our world, our relationships and our selves. However, experience is a slippery concept. It is hard to excise the precise meaning of the word from its everyday use, as if the concept of experience possessed intrinsic or self-evident meaning. The question is how can the concept of experience be used in a meaningful way? How do we know if an individual's or a community's experience is reliable? How do we know if it is true? What is truth and does it matter anyway? On the one hand, a degree of skepticism needs to be exercised if evidence is based solely on the experience of a particular community or individual. It has to be tested. On the other, there is an important place in our search for what is true, which is related to the collective experience of faith communities. This has to be tested too and other factors must hold in check the veracity of these claims. In all, I am making a modest claim for a place for experience, especially our shared experience, in the process of re-describing God in the twenty-first century.

Let's return to an earlier reflection on experience. We liked Hendrix in those halcyon days, because his edgy image and style titillated our adolescent sensibilities. But his music also touched us in the same way that great art or religious icons open up other dimensions of consciousness. Notably, the tone of his music, the tone of that wailing Fender guitar was deeply affecting. These days a cello might do the same thing for me, but in those days, the long mournful sounds of his guitar resonated deeply with my spirit. I mean spirit, not in the ghostly-disembodied sense, but more as human consciousness knows and experiences the sacred. At that time, I was not *religious*, but words like emotion or imagination seem inadequate by themselves. Obviously, there were sentimental elements, but even sentiment can bring to the surface more substantial thoughts and feelings. Without doubt, the experience and the memory of the experience were formative. Above all else, it was a shared experience. By shared experience, I do not mean that we felt the same way; rather we felt a momentary sense of connection by virtue of a common symbol, mutual friendship and close proximity. I now suspect that whatever we mean by *God* has more to do with our mutually formed experience, of being part of a network of relationships, than strict adherence to religious doctrine or formulae.

Are you experienced? This question can be examined at different levels. At one level, the question is an invitation to experience a certain kind of experience. For example, in those heady days at school, we did not do heavy drugs, make free love or play guitar, but we felt something compelling. At another level, the question is rhetorical because we are all experienced by virtue of our humanity. So, while at this stage I am not referring to God or anything explicitly religious, I am underlining the fact that the slippery concept of experience is an important part of how we interpret the meaning of our lives. Because the concept is complex, some shy away from it altogether, especially the idea of our interior or subjective experience, because it raises the issue of the emotions and the assumption that emotions have nothing to say about truth in particular and existence in general.

Experience involves a notion of awareness, of both our internal life and the external world and the connection between the two, which comes to life in community. More so, to be human is *to experience* experience, it is our awareness of our experience that makes us fully human. I spoke earlier about what it means for us to have a sense of ourselves as subjects, which is not about being isolated individuals but rather living as inter-related subjects (our mutual experience). At this level experience is the perfect term to describe how we as human subjects appropriate and express our awareness of ourselves, others and the world. While the quest for absolute certainty is elusive, if not destructive, at a practical level we function on the basis that some things are reasonably certain. It's not foolproof. In this context, our experience, especially our shared experience, teaches us about what can be relied on with a workable degree of confidence. This is wisdom for the journey.

The myth of the perfect life is disempowering and disillu-sioning, whereas the congestion zone is an apt metaphor for contemporary life that gives us permission to face and deal with life's realities. We learn to live together in the congestion zone by sometimes avoiding, bumping into and travelling with each other. There is conflict as well as moments of grace. In all this, there is an element of contingency. Experience is not an absolute, indubitable or unchanging source of knowledge, experience is contingent. I am using the term *contingency* in two ways. First, it is used in a broad sense suggesting that the quest for certainty is ultimately fruitless, because it is fraught with imponderable diffi-culties. There is always an element of doubt. Second, contingency is used in a narrower philosophical sense to say that I will not be making explicit truth claims in absolute terms. My claims are expressed in terms of probability, given certain conditions of time and place. Consequently, this means that there is also permission not to have all the answers and to live accordingly with doubt. In fact, I am arguing that a twenty-first century faith encompasses doubt and learns to live with contingency. This is the way of wisdom.

What is Truth?

A twenty-first century faith means that we are willing and able to put our wisdom, our truth and ourselves to the test. In philosophy, issues of truth are generally dealt with in the context of a theory of knowledge that deals with all sorts of things like: what is knowledge, how do you get it, what is its relationship to experience and how do you prove it is reliable or true? In a practical way, this chapter is establishing a basis for understanding how we acquire knowledge and show that it is true. However, if we grant that human existence is contingent and that faith incorporates doubt, what happens to the question of truth? When we considered the issue of religious pluralism, we recognized the reality of the plethora of diverse religious experiences. Subsequently, can we speak about truth in our multi-faceted world? It partly depends on what is meant by the concept of truth.

At this juncture, it will be helpful to re-examine fundamentalism. The purpose of this is to clarify my approach in general and in particular, what I mean by truth. It also serves to underline further the distinction between fundamentalist and mainstream Christianity. In terms of appreciating the nature of Christian fundamentalism, the question of truth is critical. I will list other identifying characteristics, but truth is pivotal. For example, while fundamentalism's presumptions are generally unfounded or unreasonable (Moses parted the Red Sea), there is an internal logic. The logic goes like this: through Jesus, God has given *the* truth exclusively to a select group and this means by inference that mainstream Christianity and other religions and philosophies do not have *the* truth. Nonetheless, the meaning of truth has been debated for centuries (Plato). Historically, there have been two extremes: absolutism and relativism. Absolutism is evident in statements like *there is one truth*. Relativism is evident in statements like *there are many truths of equal value*. However, I am proposing a third position. I am presuming that truth matters a great deal, that there are many truths but not every position is equally true and that no one possesses all the truth. In terms of Christianity, I will argue later that the life of Jesus discloses something of the truth, but not the whole truth, as our claim to truth is partial, provisional and contingent on personal, cultural and historical factors.

So what about fundamentalism and the concept of truth? Here are some of the other identifying features of Christian fundamentalism, although the list is not exhaustive. These features relate to fundamentalism's views of God, the world, the Bible, ethics and authority. First, fundamentalism maintains a form of hard theism. This means that it takes very seriously (factually and literally) the idea that God, who is outside the world, can intervene in world events. The strength of this approach is the confidence it gives in terms of prayer and guidance. Prayers will be answered (the Car Park prayer). Nevertheless, it is not clear how God intervenes or why God chooses not to intervene. What about the millions of unanswered prayers? What about the millions of innocent victims? Moreover, what about our responsibility for our own actions? For instance, the phrase "It's God's will" has been used in the past to justify all manner of exploitation, including slavery and sexism (in mainstream Christianity as well). In response, I reject hard theism and question most versions of soft theism (see below).

Second, fundamentalism interprets biblical texts literally. This process of interpretation is often referred to smugly as *the plain reading* of Scripture, where the meaning is apparently self-evident to those in the know. However, this reading is usually done in a highly selective manner. From an academic point of view, it is often not literal enough, in that it fails to examine in a systematic way the actual differences that exist between texts. For example, it fails to acknowledge the major differences that exist between the two biblical creation stories (compare Genesis 1 and Genesis 2-3) and the two accounts of the birth of Jesus (compare Matthew 1-2 and Luke 1-2). In practice, the Bible is used by fundamentalists in a highly selective manner to justify a host of positions. For instance, the majority of Christian fundamentalists would not expect women to wear veils (I Corinthians 11:6) but they would expect wives to be submissive to their husbands (Colossians 3:18). This means that fundamentalism fails to address the anomaly of justifying how, on the one hand, wearing veils is cultural and on the other hand, male headship transcends culture. This also supports the thesis that fundamentalism is a patriarchal protest movement.

In contrast, I do not have an actual/factual approach to the Bible. While the Bible is the primary source of wisdom and inspiration for Christianity, a biblical text has to be interpreted within its social and historical context.

Third, fundamentalism uses a pre-modern cosmology, like the ancient three-tiered view of the universe (hell, earth, heaven). While many mainstream churches use words like *heaven* in their worship, the meaning of *heaven* is largely symbolic, but in fundamentalism heaven is a place. Likewise, fundamentalists interpret the creation stories in Genesis as factual. Nevertheless, at least implicitly, they recognize that strict literalism poses major interpretive problems (contradictions, doublets), so they adopt a fall-back position. That is, fundamentalism sees the Bible as inerrant and hence, all the stores are *ultimately* true. This means that, regardless of the fine print, the text is factually true and that's the end of the matter.

Science poses major problems for fundamentalists, because it challenges their version of what is true (factual). For example, it is not unusual for fundamentalist Christian students to drop out of geology courses at university over the issue of the age of the earth. Nonetheless, fundamentalists will continue to try and exploit science in order to justify positions (for instance, a day in Genesis equals millions of years, or conjecture about intelligent design). In response, I am committed to working out theology in a twenty-first century context and that includes a contemporary understanding of cosmology.

Fourth, fundamentalist ethics are predominantly rule-based; expressed in legalistic terms and focused on behavior regardless of circumstances. Subsequently, moral issues are black and white. There are no shades of gray. There are only moral absolutes. For some people, unambiguous moral guidance is part of its appeal, as in "God told me that pre-marital sex is sinful".

In contrast, I reject a crude rule-based approach to complex moral issues. In the congestion zone, there are no black and white answers. Moreover, there are often competing or conflicting moral principles.

Fifth, fundamentalist truth claims are often fear based. The emphasis on fear reinforces the authority of the Bible teacher, who is the privileged interpreter of the master-narrative. Fear relates to the threat of God's punishment or the withdrawal of God's protection and increased vulnerability to attacks from Satan. Rewards are restricted to a chosen few, as in the faithful remnant, providing they accept the authority of the teacher and adhere to His teachings.

With the issue of authority, while the psychology is different, there are some similarities with the abuses of power and privilege in certain quarters of mainstream Christianity. Nonetheless, in mainstream traditions, there is also a healthy ambivalence toward authority. This is very much the case in Australia, where there is an agreed double-speak on the part of clergy and laity alike, which is evident on the occasion of the Bishop's annual parish visit, "Yes Bishop, we will do that straight away". However, after the Bishop leaves the rejoinder is "Forget it; he won't be back for a year". In contrast, I assert that grace and not fear is the motivating spirit for a twenty-first century Christianity.

This cluster of features helps to create an overall portrait of the nature of Christian fundamentalism. There are other features, like its general indifference to social justice issues. In the end, however, it is fundamentalism's attitude to truth which is arguably the defining feature of fundamentalism. For me, while the Bible is a source of inspiration, it is neither an instruction manual nor an inerrant work (Genesis 6:1-4 is a very strange text). Moreover, there is more than one truth or reading of what truth is. Because these are central issues, however, I need to elaborate further on the meaning of experience and its link with wisdom.

Experience and New Wisdom

I reject an absolutist stance on issues of truth and knowledge on the basis of the ambiguous nature of human experience. However, ambiguous experience plays a major role in contributing to knowledge and ultimately in developing an alternative understanding of God. Nevertheless, the meaning of what constitutes knowledge is debatable, especially given that philosophers themselves cannot agree about the nature and importance of issues concerning truth and knowledge. So we need to understand what we mean by knowledge in the first place, if we are going to presume to know something about God.

My understanding of knowledge does not fit neatly under a single label; this is partly because I am primarily concerned about the experience of God and the experience of the faith community. In this context, the subject matter cannot be treated in strictly objective terms. God is not an independent, observable, external *thing* and knowledge, especially where it involves new thinking about God, is not a matter of coming up with the *definitive* answer. Unlike a fundamentalist approach, I do not pretend that life is black and white or that it is possible to come up with an answer about God, humanity and the world that addresses every contingency. I also presume that the acquisition of new knowledge is incremental, which involves the gradual addition of small increases in knowledge. It is a bit by bit process and sometimes bits have to be thrown out. It is similar to what the ancients called wisdom. In the pre-modern world, the topic of wisdom covered many things, but here it refers to cumulative insights derived from the corporate experience of a faith community.

So, the accumulation of new knowledge is a bit by bit process. The question is how do all the bits fit together? The best way to explain it is in terms of three metaphors: a cable, the city of Venice and a crossword puzzle. In this context, the strength of a cable is based on the number of fibers and their interconnections, similarly with the Venice metaphor, as J. Armstrong said, "There is no solid ground upon which the city is built. But by way of millions of piers driven into the lagoon it does actually (still) stand, although no pier on its own can be thought of as uniquely supporting it". Likewise, the metaphor of a crossword puzzle functions in a similar vein. In all three metaphors, there is a sense in which knowledge is cumulative and cohesion depends on the fit between evidence, reasons and beliefs. All this presumes that no one bit in isolation represents the definitive answer, as new knowledge is partly a matter of *the fit between the bits* (though truth is not wholly captive to the fit, especially in complex ethical matters).

This kind of understanding of knowledge is an appropriate setting for talking about the place that the experience of faith communities has in new thinking about God. The idea of the relevance of the experience of faith communities covers a lot of ground. Is *all* the experience of *every* faith community relevant? Clearly, there are limits to the truth value of the experience of faith communities. By inference, this means that I am not talking about the grandiose claims made by the likes of Leroy van Bank. On this note, a number of qualifications need to be made. First, I am talking about mainstream faith communities. Second, when it comes to faith, there is no one single universal answer. Third, the discernment of new knowledge is about *the fit between the bits*. The process is dynamic. It is like a conversation between many voices: ecclesial and societal, theological and philosophical, humanistic and scientific. The experience of faith communities is one of the voices that come to life in relation to other voices (various forms of evidence, alternative traditions and explanations). The term *conversation* not only describes the process, but also gives a clue as to the nature of knowledge derived from faith communities. For even with matters of faith, truth and knowledge have social and public dimensions. Some philosophers argue that the conversation is everything. But it is not an either/or issue. On the one hand, the concept of conversation does not by itself justify belief. On the other hand, the idea of a conversation reduces the risk of treating an individual belief as a discrete and independent *bit* of evidence.

Lastly, truth claims are expressed here in probability-like statements. This does not mean anything like the exactitude of mathematical calculations, because an element of doubt is both acceptable and unavoidable. Therefore, the experience of faith communities represents an important bit of knowledge. It is a voice that needs to be heard. So, are we in a position to say what we mean by the word experience?

In general, the meaning of the word *experience* includes putting to the test, proof by trial, an interior state of being or personal knowledge. There is also a technical side, where experience is associated with observation and sense experience. In philosophy, experience is traditionally associated with the kind of knowledge that is derived on the basis of sense experience (as in empiricism). In its naive form, empiricism reduces experience almost exclusively to sense experience and presumes that there is a simple correlation between the object *out there*, sense experience and human perception.

In contrast, I am using a broader concept of experience, which includes not only sense experience but also our internal senses and introspection. Our apprehension of pain and our expression of emotions are two examples of this broader notion of experience. Indeed, there is a growing move toward recognizing the role of emotion in the discernment of knowledge.

In brief; experience is used here in two senses. The first sense of experience is described as the objective sense, for example, historical information about the life-setting of Jesus in first century Palestine. The second sense of experience is described as the subjective sense, for example, the testimony of early Church faith communities as expressed in the Bible or the Church's tradition. I do not use this second or subjective sense of experience to justify beliefs, without additional qualification and support. For example, in all likelihood no amount of testimony will convince me that Jesus *actually* walked on water (Mark 6:47-52), because such an event does not stand up to what we know about these things historically, scientifically or experientially. What really matters here is the point, the wisdom, the *existential* insight of this remarkable story (which is brimful of primal images of presence and absence). It is truly a *life in the congestion zone* story. So, the subjective sense of experience is not necessarily true or justifiable in itself and the value of its contribution depends on its interaction with other voices (other bits) in community and wider society.

In the congestion zone, experience is messy. While it is hard to describe, it is the way we engage and express our engagement with ourselves, others and the world. In this chapter, I have examined experience from three perspectives: the Church's approach to experience, our everyday understanding of experience, and questions of truth and knowledge. While the concept of experience is difficult to define, it has objective and subjective dimensions. It can be expressed in and shaped by language. It is belief-like in character. It can be expressed in the form of propositions; though knowledge in the real world is more than a series of abstract propositions as it depends on experiential support and reasons all working together. Experience by itself does not necessarily justify belief. It depends upon how it resonates with other factors. For example, an individual could passionately claim, "I began to believe in God when I experienced inner power". However, strength of conviction is only one factor. So experience, even subjective experience, has a role in justification, providing it is interpreted critically in the light of wider social and cultural experience and in conjunction with the use of reason, other evidence and is coherent with other beliefs.

CHAPTER 4

I MET GOD IN BERMUDA

In my early years at university, while consuming endless cups of coffee and smoking roll-your-own cigarettes in the small cafe as we discussed everything from sex to football, it was fashionable to celebrate the victory of absence. I now want to claim the fleeting and transforming experience of the presence of God in the world. While suffering and the silence of God has to be acknowledged, it is the experience of presence that enables us to survive, and in some cases thrive with dignity and courage. But what is this presence? In some academic circles, the idea of presence has lost all credibility. In contrast, I am making a case for presence. In the process, I am introducing two old German shepherds Paul Tillich and Karl Rahner as they have some valuable insights into presence and absence.

The Gift of the Morning

It was a warm day, the sky was blue and we were in Bermuda for the next stage of our Grand Tour. Not half bad. In the past, Mark Twain was a frequent visitor to this small, engaging sub-tropical island situated about a thousand miles north east of Miami. By the way, Michael Douglas and Catherine Zeta-Jones live here and so we agreed beforehand that, if we bumped into them, we would treat them like normal people. That morning, however, we caught a ferry from the main center of Hamilton, and headed in a north-westerly direction to the old Royal Naval Dockyard, which is on the western tip of the island. After a brief stay we caught another ferry, a small one this time, and travelled back along the northern shore toward St George, which is at the eastern end of the island. We were the only passengers on board. The sea was still, perfectly still. We glided effortlessly over the water, which was liquid-glass of an indescribable blue. The color was extraordinary. We kept looking at it, gazing, pondering, what word would do justice to the color? Azure, maybe? Anyway, it's that distinctively warm-blue Bermudian water.

From memory, our voyage took an hour. At the end of it, we were different people. There was no lightning or thunder, but we were different. It was an epiphany, which is an ironic description these days because, while no one admits to being religious, everyone seems to be having epiphanies. Like all epiphanies, it was a gift, the gift of the morning. But there was more to come.

At St George, we went to the little church of St Peter, with its light grey walls and brilliant white trim borders (established 1612). Venturing inside we met Edith, an African-Bermudian octogenarian. We chatted with her about all sorts of things, including why young people were leaving the Church. Her manner disarmed us. Edith was calm, softly spoken. Her counte-nance gave the clear impression that she had seen *everything*. Nothing would shock her, because wisdom lived here. Edith was the kind of person who made you want to say something inane like, "Please join us for lunch; we want to hear your story". We left reluctantly with, dare I say it, a sense of blessing. By blessing, I do not mean the hocus-pocus variety that cures backache and baldness and makes you fabulously wealthy. No, it had to do with how we felt, how we saw ourselves and the world. Yes, I met God in Bermuda.

The Bermuda experience was a gift as we felt that we had discovered something of the presence of God. Not for the first time and hopefully not for the last. By saying the G-word, I do not mean the fundamentalist's wrapped-in-the-clouds God or the philosophical theologian's God, who is this curious *ground of being*. On the contrary, I suspect a twenty-first century God is found in the web of relationships: human, biological and cosmo-logical. The network of relationships is the twenty-first century place for epiphanies of all persuasions and varieties. Let me explain.

In Bermuda, there was no lightning and thunder assailing us from without, but the propitious meeting of sky, water, color and Edith's presence and our selves were all of a piece. Yes, like a sacrament, which evoked an experience of the sacred from within. Let me take this further. Let me say a bit about *my* God and engage in some speculation about the future of God.

I do not expect to solve the God-problem (besides, it cannot be solved like a mathematical equation). As soon as we say that we can observe or measure or test God, then we are no longer talking about God. Nevertheless, this does not mean we cannot say something meaningful or intelligent about God, and more impor-tantly, about our experience of God. While there are many ways to re-think and re-describe God, I will be arguing that whatever we claim about God is at best a modest claim. I am not preparing the way for a bigger, brighter and better master-narrative: that is, the story that ends all stories. The presumption is that, with due deference to the contingency of human existence and the mystery of God, a redescription of God will always be incomplete and short-lived. Nothing is certain.

This is not pessimism, but wisdom as the quest for absolute certainty is exhausting and futile. Things change, we change and all this is the stuff of faith. Further, such a re-description presumes that God-talk is metaphorical; even such eminent words as king, sovereign and judge are metaphors.

Nevertheless, we still should put any description of God to the test and the test goes like this. In the twenty-first century, does the re-description make a modicum of sense in the face of the reality of suffering? In summary, the locus for redescribing God is neither the God-up-there nor the God-beneath-the-surface, the locus is here in the world (bearing in mind, it is difficult to talk about God without using spatial terms, so even the word *locus* is used metaphorically). New metaphors for God will find their home in our experience of the network of relationships, expressed in and through language, by people of good faith and faith communities who know full well the power of presence and absence.

In everyday conversations, the meaning of the concepts of presence and absence is relatively clear: for instance: Sally is here or not here, Fred is alive or dead, Rachel is in class or playing hooky. But when it comes to God, while we know something of the meaning and experience of the absence of God, what does it mean to say that God is present? That God is here? Certainly, we do not mean anything like the old man in the sky is in the living room. No, remember we are looking for a new way to think about God and the meaning of presence. Further, even when we say Sally, Fred or Rachel is here, that is, that they are present, what does that mean? Sure, there is a sense in which we *have* them. For a moment they are ours. But do we really have them?

On that beautiful morning in Bermuda, the sky and sea, the place and the company of others, conspired to evoke an experience of presence. It was disarming, delightful and nurturing. But that exquisite moment was soon gone, and while the memory of the experience is comforting, it is tinged with regret, because we cannot go back and re-live the experience or bring it back to life in the here and now. It is absent. A divine encounter has a certain humor, irony, even pathos, but above all, there is a poignancy, which derives from the reality that every divine encounter is transitory. While the Bermuda morning was a powerful experience of presence, we cannot purchase, possess or subdivide the moment of presence. Presence is not a thing. It is an encounter. The experience of presence is fleeting.

To illustrate, the biblical encounter between the iconic figure of Moses and God of the burning bush is an apt metaphor of the ambiguous experience of God. It comes close to the style and mood of a twenty-first century faith "the bush was blazing, yet it was not consumed" (Exodus 3:2). God is simultaneously present and absent. The ambiguity in this story is cause for humility with our contemporary God-talk and theological claims. Without presence, religion is empty ritual and without absence, religion is idolatrous (Golden Calf, Exodus 32). Empty ritual and idolatry, in any form, is the stuff of bad religion. What is more, the problem with theism is that it inevitably runs the risk of being, at least implicitly, a form of idolatry, as we try to control the ambiguous experience of the presence and absence of God.

Remember, Moses took his shoes off because he was on holy ground. In the midst of divine experience, rather than take our shoes off, we often trample about the place manufacturing doctrine, ritual, cleaning rosters and fundraising events. I am not against institutional forms of religion *per se* because, under the right conditions, institutions can ably and creatively serve human community and spiritual development. But I am against bad religion, where institutional forms become tyrants of the soul and consequently, we lose that surprising and destabilizing sense of divine encounter.

Overall, I am trying to provide a few broad brush strokes for a twenty-first century re-description of God. It is a restrained piece of work, in terms of its aspirations, in that it will not solve the God problem or lead to the discovery of new and defining metaphors for the twenty-first century. But I will make a case for revisiting the old metaphors of presence and absence and using them to breathe new life into the way we think about experience, God and the figure of Jesus. That is, new elements of a twenty-first century redescription of God will be found by thinking about absence and redefining presence in relation to absence. But there is a major obstacle, namely, the problem of what I call *hard* theism.

To assist us with the task of removing this obstacle, I want to introduce an important pair of concepts. In religious studies, it is common to describe spiritual encounters in terms of immanence and transcendence. The term *immanence* relates to a sense of the intimacy or the nearness of the divine, while the term *transcendence* relates to a sense of the grandeur or the incomprehensible remoteness of the divine. For example, an immanent experience can occur in the company of good friends, while a transcendent experience can occur in solitude while gazing at the stars.

Our time with Edith was an immanent experience of the sacred, whereas the blue water of Bermuda had elements of immanence and transcendence. Historically, the pair of concepts, immanence and transcendence, reflects something of the complex and unresolved debate about the nature of God and God's relationship to the world. Theoretically, they represent two different approaches to the problem of the God-world relationship. However, I am using them in a general way to describe the range of possible human responses to the sacred. Specifically, they will be used to help us understand the different ways of looking at God.

The God-World Relationship

The challenge for us is to speak meaningfully about the presence of God in a twenty-first century world. However, speaking meaningfully about God is hard enough, let alone speaking about the presence of God. The two issues are related. For instance, a discussion about the attributes of God will encroach on a discussion about how God is experienced in the world.

It is partly the difference between the God of the philosophers and the God of the theologians. From a philosophical perspective, there are many issues at stake ranging from the attributes of God to the agency of God, where agency is concerned about whether or not we can say God has the capacity to act or do or cause or intervene. In addition, the laws of logic complicate the question of God's agency; as the philosopher Richard Swinburne put it, "Can God change the rules of logic can he make $2 + 2 = 5$, or make a thing exist or not exist at the same time, or change the past?" The problem of free will also influences what can be said about what God can do or know.

From a theological perspective, concerns about the nature of God-talk have changed greatly since World War II in general and the 60s in particular. Primarily, the basis of God-talk has been challenged. Subsequently, there is wide a range of opinions now as to the meaning of the presence of God in the world. The range includes biblical, early Church, Augustinian, Thomistic, Reformation, liberal, orthodox, feminist, Asian and African-American perspectives. The presence of God has also been addressed under headings like the Kingdom of God, the Trinity or the Holy Spirit. Collectively, all these issues represent a serious challenge to traditional theism.

While my focus is on the experience of God, it would be helpful at this juncture to present thumb-nail sketches of three broad ways of describing the relationship between God and the world. To clear up possible misunderstandings, the concept of theism is not a bad thing. While I am personally not wedded to theism, I am indebted to it. Moreover, there are many versions of theism and not all of them can or should be reduced to caricature (like the Car Park God). In general, theism is a radical affirmation of both God's involvement in the world *and* the transcendence of God over and above the world.

In this context, the emphasis is more on the importance of divine revelation than human reason. The appeal of theism is that it affirms God's freedom and God's holiness and it is thus a ready antidote to the contemporary tendency to apprehend the divine for the sake of our *ready to wear* world. In the Christian tradition, spirituality is not a fashion accessory and so God cannot be purchased and displayed at our leisure. The problem with theism, however, is the task of trying to maintain both God's *separation from* and *involvement in* the world. Serious exponents of theism are the first to admit these complexities. They accept the limits. Besides, they worship God and not their own model of what God is supposed to be like.

Hard theism is the variant of theism that overlooks the inherent limits of the fact that theism is only a model of the God-world relationship. Hard theism is a *factual* interpretation of God, which mistakenly sees its *conception* of God as God's self. In that sense, it is implicitly a form of idolatry. Typically, with hard theism, God *actually* creates the world and has the capacity to intervene. God *actually* controls events in history, from traffic congestion in London to cyclones in Bermuda. This God is in charge, as a heavenly king or judge. This is the Monty Python view of God (*Monty Python and the Holy Grail*). This God is like a puppeteer who creates the stage and the puppets and then pulls the strings. In this context *the Car Park God* is not a caricature but an apt metaphor for the God of hard theism.

Nevertheless, while this form of theism emphasizes the transcendence of a God who supposedly brings order and security, it leaves many questions unanswered. What about suffering and natural disasters? What about free will? How can a good and all-powerful God let these things happen? In comparison, *soft theism* is form of theism that is more reserved in its claims. While it wants to maintain a notion of God as separate from the world, it accepts the inherent limits of its own model and explicitly interprets the God-world relationship more symbolically than factually.

There are two leading features in most versions of hard theism. First, God directly *causes* things to happen in the world. Second, God is *personal* yet remains *separate* from the world. This is the tension between wanting to claim God as *my* God and recognizing that God cannot be put in a box. Soft theism recognizes some of the problems here and has God working indirectly or symbolically in order to realize (in the sense of cause) God's purposes in the world. Nevertheless, it remains to be seen how successful soft theism will be, as it tries to remedy the shortcomings of its sibling and retain its notion of God's distinctiveness. By the way, it is interesting to note the number of Christian philosophers who promote and defend versions of hard theism that their theological counterparts abandoned long ago.

In *deism*, God creates the world but does not intervene. In this context, the emphasis is more on human reason than divine revelation (by observing nature, we make the induction that there is a *designer* God). God is like a watchmaker, who makes the watch, winds it up and stands back and watches. God is not in direct control and there is room for free will and human account-ability.

There is no immediate clash with science. But what impact, if any, does God have in personal terms? Is it meaningful to talk about the immanence of God? There are alternative versions of deism, which envisage nature as locus of the divine. However, we do not necessarily need a God to understand the workings, or appreciate the mystery of nature. While deism has space for the capacity and exercise of free will, there is not much room for God. It is arguably a *de facto* capitulation to absence.

In the nineteenth century, in particular, deism helped many scholars, poets and writers to be explicitly rational and progressive, while remaining nominally religious. Finally, *panen-theism* refers to generally more recent understandings of God's relationship to the world. In these models, the world is *in* God (unlike pantheism, where the world *is* God).

In summary, theism, deism and forms of panentheism are various ways of interpreting the nature of God and the God/world relationship. However, ultimately God *is* not theist, deist or panentheist. These are human constructs. They are devised for the purpose of understanding. With little success and even less agreement, philosophers and theologians have been thrashing out these issues for centuries. Some scholars have wisely reminded us of the limitations of our categories and pointed to a new theological future. This is partly what is intended by Tillich when he talks about the God above the God of theism.

In a similar vein, other scholars can see a future for religion, if and only if we move beyond theism and atheism. After all, if God is mystery, then it seems strange to attribute so much to God; in particular, the idea of agency. Why is it that God has to create or do anything in order to be God, if only because we have defined God as the divine doer or the first cause? What on earth do we expect from God? In general, I am presuming a panentheist model in which the presence of God is encountered in the web of relationships or the web of relationships is in God. In particular, I am more interested in exploring our *experience* of God than defining the *nature* of God, although the two aspects are not mutually exclusive. On that note, the experience of the absence of God is pivotal and inevitably, the question of absence raises itself painfully in the midst of suffering. It is important now to explore the issues of suffering and absence.

Only a Question of Suffering

The danger with analysis in a limited space is oversimplification for the sake of clarity. This is particularly true with an account of a complex concept like theism. In fairness, there is no doubt that historically, versions of theism have served faith communities well. Take for example the liturgy and architecture of the middle Ages. In a time when the ordinary person lived in fear of the invisible world, as well as the obvious dangers of the visible one, life was short and brutish. Therefore, the idea of a God who transcended the chaos of the world and promised a sense of order and security was no doubt reassuring. Typically, the need for order was expressed in the vaulting of Gothic cathedrals. It was also articulated in its highly structured worship that focused on the High Altar, which was situated at the liturgical East (because the sun/Son rises in the east). It is no wonder then that metaphors like sovereign were used to describe God in such a time and for such a world (note the language and the structures also legitimated feudal power and privileges). Moreover, it was perfectly obvious that a divine sovereign resided in the heavens because of the combination of sky as a metaphor of transcendence and a pre-modern understanding of cosmology. Therefore, I am not intending to take a cheap shot at theism.

Versions of theism were comparatively appropriate in the pre-modern period, but we are now in the twenty-first century. There are a myriad of problems associated with using a pre-modern understanding of God in a twenty-first century world. It's like an apocryphal family story of ours about my uncles Mick and Dick (these are their real names). Mick and Dick were brothers. When they were children, they wanted to fly. So they climbed up on to the garage roof, umbrellas in hand, and jumped. Apparently, arms were broken, though I am not sure how many. Subsequently, the story of Mick and Dick is the perfect metaphor for the kind of ingenuousness involved in maintaining literally a pre-modern explanation in a postmodern world. It is like trying to prove the world was created in six days. It's the kind of thinking and practice that emerges from following the Car Park God. This is the God of hard theism. It makes otherwise sensible people jump off the garage roof. If it does not work out, the people concerned either put it down to God's will and refuse to accept personal responsibility for their actions, or blame themselves for a lack of faith. In the end, however, suffering represents the acid test of theism.

Years ago, after a group discussion on the implications of our views of God, a member of the group asked somewhat dismissively, "Is it only a question of suffering?" As if to say, well apart from the issue of human suffering and natural disasters, the God of hard theism is okay. I was surprised.

In addition to the intellectual problems I have with the old man in the sky, there is a question of moral integrity. Human suffering cannot be dismissed or minimized as God's collateral damage. Most of us, directly or indirectly, can put names and faces to the countless fatalities of history. I remember painfully the death of Tom. He was 60 years of age, a diabetic and a heavy smoker. As a young priest, I visited Tom regularly over a two year period. On the surface, Tom was stoical. He could be gruff; but he had a dry sense of humor that would sneak up on you. He was capable of great warmth and candor. Almost in spite of himself, Tom's humanity shone through and lit up the room.

There were times when Tom would speak frankly about his experience of dying and his imminent death. In this frame of mind, Tom expressed deep regret about his family. He felt that he had failed them abysmally. More often than not, Tom and I engaged in animated conversations about football, politics, religion and relationships. We also played chess. I was a terrible player, whereas he was a good player and a gracious winner. Playing chess enlivened our discussions, like the prized conversations a parent shares with a teenager travelling in the car, which otherwise would not happen. Like good ritual, it created space for intimacy, even immanence. Eventually, Tom died of renal failure. It was expected; yet I was taken aback at how intensely I felt his loss. It hurt like hell. And God? Yes, the great God was silent. Nevertheless, my relationship with Tom had been the space where an experience of presence was born. It was transient, but precious. It changed me and the way I thought about Tom, life and death.

So, "Is it only a question of suffering?" The answer is yes! Of course, there are other considerations. But in terms of human decency, let alone the trustworthiness of Christianity, suffering is the main game. If we treat suffering as an unpleasant form of pre-match entertainment or a seedy sideshow, then we have failed the memory of Tom. We owe the Toms of the world, an unreserved and transparent honesty about life, death and faith.

The experience of suffering raises the toughest of all questions about the nature of God and God's relationship with the world. Specifically, the issue of suffering is a philosophical conundrum; namely, can God be all-powerful and loving? The death of six million Jews in the Holocaust is arguably *the* test case. On the one hand, if an all-powerful God let this happen, then this God is not a God of love but a monster.

On the other hand, if God is a God of love, then God would have intervened, unless of course God is not all-powerful. In response to this challenge, the counter-argument is often made that God, who is loving *and* all-powerful, has chosen to give us the gift of free will. Therefore, suffering is the price of free will. But this seems too neat, too self-satisfied and it presumes that God expects millions of people to suffer in order to validate God's magnanimous gift of free will. What a gift. What a price. What an expectation. In this context, God is a monster by another name.

The free will argument also fails to address the issue of natural disasters. Our free will is largely irrelevant in relation to the looming threat of an approaching tsunami. Further, there is another counter-argument that claims we cannot condemn God for horrendous suffering, because there is a greater mystery here that we cannot pretend to comprehend. The inference is that the significance of these losses is somehow minimized or transcended by the inestimable mystery of God. With the passage of time, this may be half right, but only half, because in the face of suffering it's *all* wrong. In what conceivable way can the Holocaust be redeemed, intellectually, morally or spiritually? While people and nations may work together to prevent new Holocausts, and in doing so the memory of the Holocaust is respected, the *actual* Holocaust cannot be rehabilitated. Furthermore, to say "God knows better" is cold comfort to the innocent victims and the survivors of history. It trivializes their suffering and demonizes God.

Besides, it does not ring true. It sounds like the edict of a parent who responds smugly to a protesting child with, "I am sorry, but that's the way it is. You'll thank me for this when you are older."

Many Christians outgrow hard theism. This is not necessarily the result of doing a five week course on the inner journey or reading a self-help book or listening to a riveting sermon. We are usually dragged into the next stage of our spiritual growth kicking and screaming. The timely course, book or sermon may help after the event, but it usually takes a crisis and the ensuing wilderness period to crystallize new awareness.

More than anything, suffering forces us to outgrow the childhood images of God. For a child, *the old man in the sky* can be synonymous with Father Christmas, the Easter Bunny, the Tooth Fairy, mum, dad, the school teacher and the new best friend, all rolled into one protective pantheon. As a child, this pantheon can be psychologically appropriate and emotionally reassuring, as if to say, "God's in his Heaven/All's right with the world!" However, the child's inner world has a complexity of its own and is not restricted to an old man in the sky. Over the years, I have encouraged children to draw pictures of *their* God and this has revealed an extraordinary diversity and plasticity of images. My hunch is that if a child, who is moving into adolescence, does not continue to develop psychologically and spiritually then the diversity and plasticity of images is reduced and set in concrete. Moreover, without the aid of a crisis, adolescents and adults can remain captive to a Father Christmas God. Inevitably, the task for adults is to re-discover faith by developing an adult view of God. We are not all the same and in maturity, there are many ways of envisaging faith.

In the end, I am advocating that seeing the experience of God as ambiguous, as presence and absence, can be an important part of adult faith exploration. Nonetheless, the idea of using the concept of presence has its critics.

Excursion, Presence: Theologians have challenged the idea of the presence of God, for example the so-called *death of God* theologians protested against theism. They grounded their theology in the experience of absence. They were not so much challenging the existence of God as responding to the perceived failure of theism. Like *death of God* theologian Thomas Altizer, who was addressing the problem of theism, arguing against *the old man in the sky* in favor of total or radical presence of the divine in the world. However, it is not clear how this works. Others raised concerns about classical theism from different perspectives. For Moltmann, suffering, and the absence of God, compels us to re-interpret the nature of God, "The murder of the Jews was an attempt to murder God". Subsequently, Moltmann addresses the question of suffering and the nature of God and by inference the question of absence is raised. Thus, Altizer and Moltmann react in different ways to theism. However, they do not represent a strictly postmodern position. In spite of his critique of theism, Altizer's concept of "total presence" is modern in its construction. As a comparison, M.C. Taylor approaches absence from a genuinely postmodern perspective. With Taylor, there is only absence. In a practical way, absence means *sheer* absence as opposed to either God's vacuum or God's hiddenness.

The Problem with Presence

The idea of presence has been widely criticized of late, as part of a movement away from the use of metaphysics. What on earth is metaphysics? Before the fog descends, let me explain. Have you ever had an earnest friend called Neville, who is always asking ill-timed questions about the meaning of life? Imagine you are with friends enjoying pasta and drinking a big red from the Napa Valley. As a chorus of delight goes around the table for this fruity, but not precocious cabernet sauvignon, Neville disturbs the genial atmosphere by asking "But what does it mean?" Invariably, someone replies with annoyance, "Neville, it's just a very nice glass of wine!" Neville cannot help himself, as he becomes more earnest and pleads, "I know it's a nice glass of wine, but what does it *really* mean?" In the end, Neville is asking a metaphysical question. Metaphysics is interested in meaning. It is interested in how the world *really* is. But that raises all sorts of questions.

Some philosophers would speculate about "the ideal wine" or "the ideal of wine". Some would say dismissively, "It is a glass of wine and that is the end of the matter". Still others would counter with "Yes it is a glass of wine, but it is fascinating that it exists in the first place". Now here comes the metaphysical rub. Existence has been a source of fascination for many, and in the right setting, Neville's questions are good questions. However, it is one thing to say that the glass of wine exists and it is quite another thing to say that there is more to this glass of wine than meets the eye.

It is shaky ground to respond to Neville's curiosity and wonderment by speculating that there is in fact something deeper and broader called existence (or being or God), which is a thing or is thing-like or if it is not thing-like it transcends the physical qualities of the glass of red wine. Okay, we could say the color red is universal but that is not the same as saying it has a life of its own.

This is the crux of the metaphysical debate. Typically, metaphysical approaches explain what is happening in the world before our eyes, by reference to some kind of universal idea, quality or essence which lies beyond our immediate experience.

In terms of presence, there is the metaphysical tradition of platonic Christianity, as Nietzsche said, "We godless anti-metaphysicians still take our fire, too, from the flame lit by a faith that is thousands of years old, that Christian faith which was also the faith of Plato, that God is the truth, that truth is divine". The metaphysical bent means that rather than treat the meaning of an object or text at face value, we go beyond the object or text and refer to being, God or some higher *external* source of authority for the purpose of explaining our beliefs.

It is part of the quest for the grounds of certainty. As one scholar put it, its motivation has to do with an individual or community binding itself securely, "with a stable, knowable super-object". It's like when, as a child; your big sister corrects your errant behavior by saying, "Because Dad said so" in order to justify her position. In both cases, metaphysics and the big sister, the implication is that Dad is in the next room and he can be called upon any time for reassurance and support. Of course, in this case, we can at least inspect the next room in order to verify the presence of Dad.

In short, why can't we enjoy a glass of red wine without having to justify the experience as a manifestation of something that is beyond our experience? This is a reasonable question.

Likewise, a conception of the presence of God that relies on metaphysics is equally open to a multitude of challenges. Therefore, while I accept that the question of the meaning and relevance of metaphysics has not been resolved, I will leave those considerations in Neville's hands. Subsequently, it is important to establish the credibility of the idea of presence and it is my intention to use presence in a post-metaphysical manner (that is, without the aid of explicit metaphysical speculation).

Excursion, Deconstruction: I am interested in re-describing God in terms of presence and absence. While I want to claim a place for absence, I also want to articulate a vision of presence. The two go hand-in-hand. Moreover, the current interest in absence is often linked to a broad intellectual movement known as deconstruction, which is associated with the philosopher Derrida, who challenged the metaphysics of presence. In this light, an argument can be made that language about the presence of God is a remnant, a mark or a trace and ought not to be confused with the *actual* presence of God. However, deconstructionism is only one of many postmodern perspectives and not all scholars embrace it with equanimity. It also has its critics. In particular, it has been accused of neglecting major philosophical traditions (like Wittgenstein's work on language). In short, postmodernism means more than deconstruction as it also entails a number of other disciplines, styles and values. Nevertheless, the combined critique of presence cannot be dismissed lightly.

Presence and Everyday Life

Presence needs reclaiming for our era, which is why I am developing a post-metaphysical view. So, what would presence look like in the twenty-first century? In the present era, absence is presumed and the onus of proof is on presence.

There are many reasons in favor of the absence of God in the world. First, the God master-narrative, the story to end all stories, has been challenged historically, theologically and philosophically. Second, the God master-narrative does not hold in the light of the experience of suffering (Auschwitz). Third, the metaphysical foundations of presence have been shaken. In modernity, God is absent partly because God is interpreted as non-sensible or non-factual (ie. God is not a *thing*). Generally, this means that there is no concrete evidence that can be summoned to support the claim that God is present in the world. God is absent because there is no *objective* proof to say that God is present. So, God is absent by default.

In postmodernity, the issue is more complicated. For a start, the question of what constitutes reliable evidence is debatable. For instance, in modernity, God is absent because God is designated as spiritual and the world as material and the spiritual and material are defined as different and separate. In the present era, the lines are blurred and there is any number of possibilities. It may be that, God is absent because the philosophical foundations of theism have been discredited. Alternatively, God may be present but there are now alternatives, even competing gods.

I intend to take a postmetaphysical view of presence. I mean three things by the term *postmetaphysical*. First, it means that I will not revert to terms like *being* to justify my position, though this is hard to do because words like *God, Jesus, Spirit, Church* and *sacrament* have a history saturated with metaphysical associations. Second, there are many models and metaphors for God and the God/world relationship. This is a complex issue. However, I am concentrating on the experience of God. Third, I do not presume that the pair, presence and absence, encompass the whole meaning of the human experience of God. It is tempting to make this claim, but this would run the risk of homogenizing the diverse and ambiguous experience of God.

Further, not only will I redefine presence, but I will give absence equal air time. Indeed, the key to appreciating my understanding of God is found in the ambiguity of experience as presence *and* absence. There are also social grounds for reclaiming presence. Finally, there is an anomaly in that, while experience is eagerly summoned to argue in favor of absence, experience of presence is often looked upon with suspicion.

Therefore, I am claiming that, while the argument from experience is not conclusive by itself, it has a place in the process of the discernment of new knowledge. No matter how slippery the concept of experience is, experience is what we know, as it registers and discloses the enduring pain of absence and the fleeting joy of presence.

My main argument is based on the ambiguous experience of God in the world, where ambiguity cannot be resolved and is understood in terms of presence *and* absence. The concept of ambiguity is not used here to imply that the meaning is vague, but rather that there is more than one meaning. In the experience of an event, different people interpret the meaning of experience differently. An object, another person or an event elicits multiple meanings. Thus, ambiguity is defined in relation to the experience of God and as such ambiguity has two interrelated meanings: presence *and* absence. Moreover, I assert that presence and absence are integral parts of the experience of God in the world. Both are needed to constitute the full meaning of the experience of God as ambiguity is part and parcel of contingent human existence. This is in keeping with, what the sociologist Zygmunt Bauman describes as, "the postmodern awareness of no certain exit from uncertainty".

Life is not neat and neither is our experience of God. An understanding of the somewhat messy nature of life and the ambiguous nature of religious experience, gives us permission to redescribe and rediscover a faith fit for the twenty-first century. The bottom line is that the mess cannot be tidied up and the ambiguity cannot be resolved.

Our two German shepherds, Tillich and Rahner, knew this intuitively. In their era, they took these issues seriously and they both have something to contribute, especially concerning the ambiguous nature of the experience of God in the world. So, who are they? For a start, they are both major twentieth century figures. In biographical terms, there are a number of differences between the two theologians. Tillich (1886-1965) came from an upper class Prussian Lutheran home, whereas Rahner (1904-1984) came from a middle class Alemanian Catholic home. Unlike Rahner, Tillich experienced warfare firsthand. Tillich enjoyed celebrity status, especially in America, while Rahner was a comparatively reserved person. Tillich was free of the constraints of anything like the *magisterium* (the teaching office and authority of the Catholic Church); whereas Rahner believed a theological conception ought to respect the *magisterium*.

There is, however, a strong family resemblance between our two theologians. This exists partly because they emerged from a similar European intellectual environment. They witnessed similar historical events (for example, the rise of National Socialism). They shared similar apologetic concerns. They shared the concern that the Christian faith ought to be accessible, relevant and life-giving. They had similar theological and philosophical interests, ranging from the importance of experience to an appreciation of symbol. They used similar sources. Above all they both responded creatively to the challenges of modernity by addressing human experience. Significantly, their similarities, as well as their differences, have not been explored at length in theology. But how do they measure up in terms of my interest in the ambiguity of experience?

The focus is Tillich's and Rahner's views on presence and absence. To appreciate Tillich, it is important to recognize his creativity as well as his repeated failure to define clearly his key terms. Part of Tillich's appeal is found in his creative use of language and his insight into the tragic side of existence. In his own way, Tillich is a modern metaphysical poet (but I do not mean rhyming couplets).

In terms of his view of God and the world, Tillich's world is essentially flawed. It is a broken world. It is this sense of the fragmented nature of human existence that lends his writing pathos. So much so that the individual in Tillich is something of a lone hero, *a la* film noir, teetering on the brink of existence, who in spite of a legion of personal doubts, summons the courage to be. In terms of presence and absence, Tillich describes the absence of God metaphorically as the vacuum that kindles in us a sense of longing for presence and this space is God's space, because only God can fill it. In this space, God is not absent because the Spirit is present. However, the absence of God is experienced by humankind as emptiness. According to Tillich, "we feel His absence as the empty space that is left by something or someone that once belonged to us and has now vanished from our view".

The significance of absence is patently clear in his work on estrangement (alienation, separation). For Tillich, estrangement means there is in-built rift between our selves and the world, and in the end, this marginalized existence means we lose a sense of who we are and where we belong. Thus, the absence of God, in Tillich, is a symptom of the fragility of human existence and that it is our destiny to live *on the edge*.

Tillich is not intending to say that God is *really* absent, but only that humankind experiences absence in our state of estrangement. The experience of absence arouses a yearning for God.

Moreover, the experience of God as presence and absence discloses something about the nature of God. This is evident in his use of two related terms: ground and abyss. For Tillich, *ground*, like the earth, is our metaphysical foundation, upon which we build our sense of who we are and where we belong. It makes us who we are. *Abyss*, with its primeval overtones, is like some kind of great cosmic pit of the unknown. It is the boundary situation, where we teeter between the limits of our existence and the mystery of God. All in all, we live permanently on the brink and we are constantly at risk of falling over the edge. Therefore, for Tillich, human existence is an enduring crisis.

Further, his use of the terms ground and abyss is a perfect example of his *poetry*, insight and lack of clarity. The terms *ground* and *abyss* form an inseparable pair and the interplay between them is like the poignant encounter at Bermuda. On the one hand, in Bermuda we experienced something of the presence of God. We knew we were momentarily *grounded* in the divine. However, we knew how precious and precarious an encounter with presence is. On the other hand, we experienced the absence of God, and absence is disarming because, as we approach the edge of the abyss, we move inevitably from an experience of fulfillment to profound emptiness.

Rahner's writing lacks the poetry of Tillich, but there is insight, clarity and heart (Rahner's prayers are deeply moving). In terms of his view of God, Rahner's God is a God of grace and, without discounting the reality of suffering, human existence is unified. The source of unity is found in God.

To appreciate Rahner fully, it is important to explore the nature of this unity. For him, humankind is created by a gracious God, such that humankind has an innate capacity to respond to God. This God works from the inside out. The individual discovers that everyday life induces and fosters a sense of hope and anticipation about the possibilities life has in store for us, because God is the source of unity who binds all things together. From the beginning, God has imparted (communicated) something of God's self to humankind. Therefore, humankind has a natural orientation toward God. It is a wonderful, and in some ways a contemporary anthropology, which does not dismiss the reality of evil and suffering, but articulates something of the innate dignity of humankind.

In all, this anthropology is the perfect setting for a discussion of Rahner's concept of presence. For Rahner, awareness of presence is humankind's awareness of an innate experience of God. This is the awareness of the nearness of God. Through experience, the world around us draws out the presence of God from within, bringing it to the surface of our awareness. This awareness in turn leads to a greater understanding of who we are in God. Therefore, human subjectivity, our awareness of who we are as human beings, is *the place* for an experience of the presence of God. There is no need to look to the heavens above.

Unsurprisingly, Rahner has been criticized for reducing the divine to a personal encounter, but for him a personal encounter takes place *in history*. To appreciate this, it is important to return to one of his premises, namely, we need the world around us in order to learn. For him, humankind experiences self-awareness, when it is in the presence of an object or a person, which acts like a catalyst triggering our perceptions. In other words, we cannot live, let alone thrive, in a vacuum. Thus, history is the context in which the awareness of the presence of God and the self are simultaneously summoned and acknowledged.

Further, humankind is human in a sensible mode. We are not disembodied ghosts, "we are actually human only in humanity". This is an insight into his view of the importance of our shared experience in that others are the (human) triggers that evoke a response from within us. We are human in concert with others. Our bodies, and the physical world around us, are not problems to be solved as they make human experience possible. Moreover, our responses to experience, even in seclusion, are partly shaped or pre-shaped by shared experience.

Tillich and Rahner helped put the ambiguity of the experience of God on the modern theological map. Tillich, something of an ecclesial celebrity, was on the cover of *Time* magazine on three separate occasions. Rahner, while more reserved than his counterpart, made his presence felt at Vatican II (and in its far-reaching ramifications). Significantly, they both recognized and celebrated the presence of God, while taking absence seriously. They sensed implicitly that there was something important in the interplay of presence and absence. As a couple of theological heavyweights, who in their own way strode upon the world stage, they wrestled with the messiness of human existence and the ambiguity of God. While the meaning of these things was not always clear in their work, its significance permeated their more popular works (sermons, prayers, interviews, radio broadcasts).

Suffering cannot be sidelined. It is the main game because it confronts us with the absence of God. So, to all the self-help gurus and televangelists offering seven steps or five biblical quotes to happiness, do not promise the moon when you cannot deliver, and do not inoculate us against the reality of suffering. Let's get back to the reality of suffering and the experience of absence, because it's only then that can we talk with credibility about the presence of God.

On that basis, I have developed a plausible case for the idea of presence. So let's unpack the meaning of presence as a way of drawing the various strands together. What does presence *feel* like? Well to begin with, we need to imagine a range of possible divine encounters from a sunny day in Bermuda to playing chess with an old friend (who is dying). Remember, we met God in Bermuda. It wasn't lightning and thunder, it was an experience of presence and absence.

In the end, there are no simple answers to suffering.

Nevertheless, with courage, we choose to live with dignity. This is the kind of dignity that comes from self-acceptance. By self-acceptance, I am not talking about the well-rehearsed slogans of the latest self-help book, claiming to have unique insights into the human soul, combined with the wisdom of the East that transcends the flotsam and jetsam of Western religion. Don't get me wrong, I am critiquing institutional Christianity, but I am also refusing to relinquish blindly or hastily the old religion for New Age versions of fundamentalism. With Tom, I had an experience of presence. Passing but engaging and renewing. This does not mean I don't have sad moments about Tom, because I do. However, there was a remarkable sense of letting go; and yes, moments of self-acceptance. Though absence elicits a powerful sense of loss, presence is a moment of connection, of discovery. It is brief, but it is potent.

Suffering happens. In the long run, however, it is no use blaming God. In some instances, we are clearly accountable for suffering because of the things we have done or failed to do (like Rwanda); while in other cases we are accountable because of our shared humanity (as in our response to a natural disaster).

In fact, my God is found in the very power of *shared* human experience. In the midst of shared experience, we encounter presence, gracious presence as a sense of self-acceptance, warts and all, which enables us to live with a sense of courage and a willingness to respond creatively to the human predicament. Without a sense of self-acceptance, we are permanently and pathologically stuck in our own small world.

CHAPTER 5

AN IRISH PUB OFF WALL STREET

Why bother with Jesus? The answer is that Jesus discloses in his life and actions something of the presence of God in the world. He is not the only source, but he is a profound source of presence. However, there are many obstacles that can get in the way of a new appreciation of Jesus. In this light, we need to talk about the death-resurrection event in twenty-first century terms. The key to this is the shared experience of early faith communities. Historically, this experience has been too easily dismissed as irrelevant or immaterial.

A Small Death

We met God in Bermuda. Yes, for us, it was a renewing encounter with the presence of God-in-the-world. I will try and say something a little more substantial about the character of presence in this chapter. Certainly, presence cannot be fully analyzed, because it is a fleeting encounter with what is traditionally described as the mystery of God. However, there is a danger here of bringing in the concept of *mystery* prematurely, and in so doing, short-circuiting the process of critical thinking.

In metaphorical terms, mystery is the upper limit or ground we cannot penetrate. The idea of mystery is a reminder that, while faith should be carefully scrutinized from as many perspectives as possible (human experience, critical reasoning, academic disciplines), it is not entirely the same as studying other phenomena. With this qualification in mind, much can be said about the character of presence.

An encounter with presence is transforming but fleeting, indelible but passing, overwhelming but evanescent. Above all, the encounter can be described as an experience of grace. While grace does not resolve the ambiguous nature of existence, it enables us momentarily to transcend the frailty of human existence. All this is paramount because the notion of grace is often summoned, when the going gets tough, as a comforting cure-all. It is something like, "Oh it was terrible, but it does not matter because it was a means of grace" (hence, end of argument).

Therefore, I want to make a claim for grace as characteristic of presence, but I am not suggesting in any way that the ambiguous nature of experience is less ambiguous because of grace. No. Life is ambiguous, contingent and provisional. Life can be a source of great joy and beauty, but it is tricky, vexing and plain complicated.

So grace, as a characteristic of presence, is not separate from an experience of absence or even an addition to the experience of absence. Ironically, absence prefigures grace. Absence ushers grace into the theater of human existence. On that note, let me tell you about a small death in Manhattan.

One fine spring day in New York we walked from our hotel in the Upper West Side, down Broadway, to Wall Street. To our surprise, we found the financial district deserted. This added to the sense of occasion because we felt we were entering the Holy of Holies as we ambled through this glass, steel and concrete icon of the American dream. I know it sounds ridiculous, but we were famished. In holiday mode, we had scarcely thought of lunch, so we left this sacred site and wandered down a side street in search of food. Shortly, we came to an Irish pub and climbed up a narrow stairway to the first floor and found, with the exception of the bar attendant, an empty bar. The bar attendant was staring impassively out the rear window as she mechanically wiped one glass after another. She was a young Irish woman called Mary. She came across the room to our table, listless, resigned. She half-smiled but her countenance said, "Not another customer". This made us all the more determined to engage with her.

Mary soon came to life. As she chatted away to us, we knew we had encountered a lively, intelligent and charming human being. She recognized our Aussie accents and ordered for us a big Australian Syrah (a Barossa Valley Shiraz) and a tasty quesadilla. The three of us then discussed the great mysteries of America. From the outset, we all declared our love of Americans. We loved their *can do, will do* and *what's next* attitude. While none of us fully understood the history or psychology of American foreign policy, we marveled at America's *in your face* energy, confidence and hospitality. I still miss the refrain "You're welcome". Generally, Americans take you as you are, it's like, "I don't need to know your past, just show me your stuff". Eventually, we asked Mary if she ever went back home to Ireland. But no, America is home now. After Mary had been living in the US for five years she had gone back to Ireland and her family greeted her with spite-filled barbs, "Who do you think you are living in New York". In the face of this barrage, Mary would cry out in her defense "I'm just a barmaid". Unperturbed, her family reminded Mary of her station in life, namely, she was a downstairs person "and don't you forget it". It was a painful reminder that some of the cruelest cuts in life are received, not on the battle field, but in the living room.

From the pained look on Mary's face, we knew this experience was a small death. It was a void, an absence, yes, a small death. Strangely, as we listened to Mary and as our listening encouraged Mary to speak with candor, there was a fleeting encounter with presence. It was a moment of connection, a gracious encounter that does not dismiss or trivialize suffering, but recognizes and renews human dignity. It was a moment of grace.

Captain Mendoza

Grace is a defining quality of the presence of God in the world. It is inclusive, indiscriminate and unconditional. It is here and now, in the midst of relationships, offering hope in the face of suffering. The meaning of grace is expressed superbly in a scene from the film *The Mission*. It is one of the great cinematic portrayals of an encounter with presence. The film is set in eighteenth century South America. Captain Rodrigo Mendoza, played by Robert De Niro, is a mercenary and slave trader. He is a very bad man, expert in the capture and enslavement of the Guarani Amerindians. He is at ease with violence, disconcertingly so. It is instinctive to him, so much so that Mendoza kills his brother out of jealousy. Perversely, Mendoza is urbane and charming too, in a subtle and disarming manner. Nevertheless, he is an empty man and his life is a sacrament of absence.

Six months after the death of his brother, Mendoza experiences the understated but compelling influence of Fr Gabriel, a Jesuit priest played by Jeremy Irons, which constitutes the beginnings of Mendoza's conversion experience. As a self-imposed act of penance, Mendoza returns to the heart of the rainforest with Fr Gabriel and the other priests, pulling the baggage of his past behind him. Specifically, Mendoza gathers the symbols of his former ways (breastplate, helmet, sword and musket) into an enormous bundle; the size and weight of the bundle commensurate with the burden of his old life. In a grotesque scene, he proceeds laboriously to drag the bundle by rope through the forest. The whole thing is tortuous to watch as Mendoza's face and body, his entire being, endures a wretched mix of despair and self-recrimination. Not even his pious companions can persuade Mendoza to lighten, let alone release the load. It is painful stuff.

Inevitably, the film drew me into its world, such that I was no longer a dispassionate observer. I was now in the rainforest living out my own story and naturally, I forgave him. I was aware of his past and I forgave him, but like his priest-companions, I could not offer him grace.

Finally, the pilgrims come to the bottom of a raging waterfall; seemingly an insurmountable barrier. Climbing, slipping back and stumbling forward, they eventually succeed in taming the cliff face and scramble up onto the plateau above the falls, where they encounter a group of the Guarani, the innocent ones who had previously suffered at Mendoza's hands. Both parties stand in complete, unbearable silence. Staring. A Guarani tribesman takes the initiative and advances, quietly and purposefully, with knife in hand. Mendoza, who is spent, done and compliant, is now on his knees with head bowed, waiting in confessional mode to receive due punishment. Instead, the Guarani tribesman's knife narrowly passes Mendoza's head and cuts the rope. In virtually the same liberating action, the tribesman then proceeds with clear intent to push Mendoza's bundle over the cliff face and into the waters below. As it falls, the bundle now looks small and impotent.

Mendoza begins to weep; this is the grief that comes from deep-down. Unexpectedly, he begins to laugh. The Guarani join in and together they create a chorus of elation. This is the kind of laughter that theologians describe as joy. This is not to be confused with amusement; for it comes from the same place as the tears. It does not mean everything is resolved and at last we have a happy ending. Sorrow as well as joy is here and the bitter-sweet poignancy of absence-and-presence, all expressed hypnotically in and through the haunting music of Ennio Morricone. Even though the Jesuit priests gave Mendoza comfort, only the Guarani could give him grace. Lamentably, the film ends in tragedy with a Church-sanctioned rout of the Guarani, and Morricone's music returns to underline the abject waste.

There is no joy, no life-lesson, no moral resolution or philosophical explanation; only suffering. However, there is a trace of presence as a handful of Guarani children escape and when it comes to presence; a trace is all we need.

So what is grace? It has to do with self-acceptance. The term *self-acceptance* is a trendy and overused term. In contrast, when it comes to grace, I am talking about beginning with our common, unadorned humanity. It is in the unrefined state, that self-acceptance greets us unexpectedly from within. It is a symptom of grace. This brings us to the Jesus stuff. But first, put the miracles aside.

While they once spoke powerfully to *pre*-modern Christians, they now run the risk of being unnecessary distractions, even obstacles to faith in our *post*-modern era. No, look at the person who broke the rules in the name of love. Practically, we know little about Jesus, but the theme of grace weaves its way through the stories, sayings, editorial glosses and scribal embellishments. Grace is central. It happens when we are in a screaming heap (or soon after). It is premised on the idea that we are acceptable and accepted. It is the human-side of the divine encounter. It may only happen a few times in life, yet it changes us permanently, because it changes the way we see ourselves, others and the world. In the case of Mendoza, he never forgot his past and his past could not be expunged, but he forgave himself and re-entered the human community. That's self-acceptance.

Here we have the heart of the Christian narrative. It is not ritual, dogma or neo-gothic wonders. It is grace. In the midst of absence, there is a transient yet transforming and humanizing expression of presence. And this is the Jesus story.

We see this in the parable of the lost son (Luke 15:11-32), where the dissolute younger brother returns home from the far-off country, expecting and deserving punishment, only to be welcomed and embraced by his father. Its meaning is spelled out in the Sabbath stories (Mark 3:1-5). That is, while the law prohibited work on the Sabbath, Jesus healed the sick in the name of love and in defiance of the law.

So, why bother with Jesus? It is worthwhile engaging with the figure of Jesus, because in the face of suffering and the short-comings of institutional religion, he is an irrepressible, incandescent and indestructible symbol of grace. Further, Jesus is a potent sign and expression of the presence of God in the world. This is the real world, in which people get caught up in the anguish of the human predicament, with all its disasters and delights, failures and successes. By naming and relegating the *old man in the sky* to the back blocks of history, the significance of presence as it is embodied by Jesus and his community of equals becomes clearer.

Furthermore, the key to a new appreciation of Jesus is found in embracing the ambiguity of experience. His life makes some sense of the congestion zone. His *way* speaks compassionately to the small deaths and great threats of human existence. In this context, the death-resurrection of Jesus is decisive. But first, we need to clarify issues concerning the contemporary study of Jesus.

Setting the Scene

In the first chapter, I mentioned the centrality of Jesus to Christian faith and identity. I argued that before we could give him a fair hearing, we needed to eject some baggage. The significance of this baggage is epitomized by the panic response my clerical presence provokes at wedding receptions (*the kiss of death*). Moreover, on the basis of a multitude of media items and non-fiction works, there is a sense in which Jesus is on trial in the twenty-first century. So, I use the shorthand term *the Jesus question* to capture something of the polemic surrounding his name.

On that score, I was conducting a discussion group in the mid 90s, at the champagne and smoked salmon parish of the diocese. It was known as a boutique parish because it attracted a plethora of New Age aficionados (academics, lawyers, musicians, psychologists and other professionals), who had returned to the Church looking for good worship, intellectual freedom and free champagne. The parish was endeavoring to offer an authentic, alternative and contemporary expression of Christianity. As we came to the end of the discussion, a young woman called Emma piped up with "I love the parish, but why do we bother with Jesus?"

I was gob smacked, though I tried to appear unfazed. I was not offended; it was the fact that it came from left-field that caught me by surprise. It certainly was a genuine question, as Emma was a sincere, intelligent, level-headed school teacher. She had been brought up as *a good Anglican*, but had outgrown the Sunday school God. Following university, she had travelled widely, exploring diverse lifestyles and philosophies, and returned to Australia seeking a thinking spiritual faith.

On reflection, Emma's question was on the right track. Whether it's in a local parish or a grand cathedral, the Church has to answer the Jesus question because it is bound to its identity and credibility. In this instance, the ethos of this particular parish was laudable, however, there was little to show in terms of the shape and content of this alternative Christianity. That is, the parish knew what it was rejecting, but could say little about what it was offering. At one level, being an open and hospitable faith community is all that matters, as that in itself it is a tangible expression of grace.

What is more, though it is easy to criticize both traditional theism and the Church, and many a critic has made merry out of these old chestnuts, it is hard to describe a new way forward. Nonetheless, if a redescription is to be *Christ*-ian, then we have to bother with Jesus. Yet as we know, the surest way to ruffle a cocktail party is to mention his name.

However, to put the Jesus question in present-day context, some general remarks need to be made about Jesus in biblical scholarship. In recent years, there has been a heated debate in biblical scholarship about the meaning of the historical Jesus (or the Jesus of history). The debate concerns *the quest* to find the *real* Jesus. The present quest stems in part from a group of scholars who make up what is known as *The Jesus Seminar*. This group developed a graded system for assessing New Testament texts in terms of historical reliability. They then voted on individual texts in order to arrive eventually at the *real* Jesus. All this raises issues about the academic discipline of history in general, as well as the history of Jesus in particular. Remember the earlier discussion about the problems involved in identifying and interpreting historical *facts*. Certainly, history has an important role in relation to the authentic study of religion. For example, historically the Church promoted anti-Semitism, partly because of a simplistic and one-sided interpretation of the references to "the Jews" in the Gospel of John. In comparison, history informs us that Jesus was a Jew. He was not a fair-haired Englishman. History also teaches us about the significance of Judaism. All these *facts* make us revisit and re-interpret the Gospel of John and we now recognize that the term "the Jews" has a polemical role, which discloses something of the vested interests of the writer. Specifically, the term "the Jews" has a rhetorical function like "the loyal opposition". Therefore, history is vital.

However, not everyone is happy with *The Jesus Seminar* and its use of history. Moreover, faith includes other considerations over and above historical facts. Faith is about meaning, lifestyle and relationships in the here and now. This means it has a strong experiential (subjective) component. While history is important and the facts cannot be ignored, it does not have the final say in matters of faith.

So where do we find the real Jesus? There is renewed interest in the relationship between history and the significance of Jesus. This interest comes under the broad heading of the so-called *third quest*. *The Jesus Seminar* is a conspicuous element within the third quest that has captured the public imagination. The third quest expresses something of modernity's search for certainty and its confidence in academic disciplines as diverse as architecture, history and sociology in finding *the facts*. Consequently, if the facts are known, then the Church's dogmatic propositions can be challenged and deposed. For example, B.L. Mack asserts that the importance of Jesus "as a thinker and teacher can certainly be granted and even greatly enhanced once we allow the thought that Jesus was not a god incarnate but a real historical person". In contrast, L.T. Johnson represents the other side of the debate. His somewhat over-zealous criticism of the third quest and *The Jesus Seminar* concerns the issue of historical reductionism. In his view, members of *The Jesus Seminar* are in danger of granting history absolute status. This is history as the final arbiter. This means that, in terms of new insights and knowledge, history has been granted privileged status. It's the new master-narrative, the story to end all stories.

But the discipline of history writing has its own problems. It is important to recall that the historian and the historian's social context influence the task of interpretation. This is similar to the problem Albert Schweitzer addressed a hundred years ago in relation to the first quest, "The Jesus of Nazareth who came forward publicly as the Messiah, who preached the ethic of the kingdom of God, who founded the kingdom of heaven on earth, and died to give his work its final consecration, never existed. He is a figure designed by rationalism, endowed with life by liberalism, and clothed by modern theology in a historical garb".

The idea of a quest refers to movements which applied the methods and insights of the discipline of history to biblical texts. By using these methods, they hoped to discern the real Jesus. This is the historical Jesus and not the so-called mythological Christ.

Since the nineteenth century there have been three significant quests and one major break. Notably, the formative period for the social and intellectual development of Tillich and Rahner took place during the break; that is, between the first and the second quest. This period is roughly between the end of the nineteenth century and the middle of the twentieth century. Subsequently, Tillich and Rahner were part of a theological movement that was skeptical about the promised outcomes of the quest for the historical Jesus. Specifically, they were critics of historical *reduc-tionism*. Reductionism is a key term. In general, reductionism is the process of pulling things apart in order to find out how they work. In the case of the quest for the historical Jesus, the reductionist process involves reducing biblical texts to their component parts, on the assumption that some parts are more important than others. The important parts are regarded as authentic or primary. The other parts are regarded as inauthentic or secondary glosses or additions.

Now Tillich and Rahner were critical of *unthinking* reductionism. They rejected the assumption that thinks complex sociohistorical events or figures can be reduced unequivocally into discrete bits of information (facts). For them, the meaning of biblical texts and figures is more than the sum of the *authentic* parts. It's like having pulled a car engine apart into its component parts. We now have these parts strewn over the garage floor, but the separate parts do not make an engine, let alone a car. Alternatively, a working engine is not the same as the 462 separate parts.

While Tillich and Rahner respected the achievements of historical method, their focus was on the contemporary meaning of Jesus. In practice, they distinguished between the first century Jesus of history and the ongoing significance of the Christ of faith. For Tillich, the significance of Jesus as Christ-figure is realized by faith through human participation and not by means of historical evidence or techniques. This is partly because the Jesus in the biblical text *is* the Christ of faith and but also, it is not easy to get *behind* the text to the Jesus of history.

Likewise, Rahner accepts the general findings of modern biblical studies about the life of Jesus. Nevertheless, the full significance of Christ for him can only be found by means of experience. In brief, Tillich and Rahner see the experience of faith communities in the first (and twentieth centuries) as crucial for understanding the Christian faith. For both scholars, symbols play a role in articulating the significance of the experience of faith communities.

Excursion, Uniqueness: The idea of Jesus being unique is imperative for most fundamentalist and many (traditional) mainstream Christians. While this topic demands separate and detailed treatment, it is relevant here because of its link with the issue of truth. I recognize that for many longstanding Christians, this is a delicate and sensitive issue because of its presumed link with truth. Remove this card and all the cards come crashing down. The logic is something like *faith in God is only true, if it is true that Jesus is unique.* Now, at the historical level, Jesus is unique just as Mohammed is unique. But that is not what is usually meant by those who defend the uniqueness principle.

In contrast, the issue of the uniqueness of Jesus can be a stumbling block for people pondering the Christian tradition, who, from the outside, read the claim of uniqueness as a sign of arrogance. There are also good arguments against the uniqueness claim. First, on cultural grounds it is hard to argue that, in the light of religious pluralism, his way is the only way. Second, on philosophical grounds, it is not clear why something of *universal* significance, as expressed in the life and person of Jesus, is *only* found in this one *particular* life.

Finally, the uniqueness debate is like arguing dogmatically that Picasso was better than Mozart. On what basis can we say, apart from personal preference, that Picasso's *Guernica* is better than Mozart's *Requiem*? To say "I prefer Picasso's paintings over Mozart's music" does not necessarily mean Mozart was inferior. Likewise, the fact that I choose to follow the way of Jesus, does not necessarily mean Mohammed's or Gautama's way is inferior. Conversely, the fact that others choose to follow other ways does not mean that the way of Jesus is made null and void. Importantly, for me, Jesus is the symbol, sacrament or icon of God and his way discloses the presence of God in the world. Besides, Jesus does not have to be the first, the only, the best or the biggest or the author of *the* master-narrative, for his life and teachings to be life-enhancing. Incidentally, I once led 25 parishioners through a series of inter-faith studies. We experienced things like worship in a synagogue and a day with a Buddhist monk. The overwhelming response was increased appreciation of other religions and greater clarity about what is means to be Christian.

Merely a Symbol?

Experience is important and our experience of God as presence and absence is critical. In this context, I argue that a twenty-first century redescription of God needs to account for the ambiguous nature of human experience. Experience was also important for Tillich and Rahner. Significantly, they used a modern under-standing of symbol to explain *how* people *experienced* the presence of God in the world. In general, they made extensive use in their work of symbols and how symbols work. They recognized that people use symbols all the time in everyday life. Moreover, these personal symbols, in terms of the dynamic of how a symbol works, share something in common with the shared and historic symbols of the Church, like the cross or the sacraments.

The pivotal idea was that symbols are powerful for us, because we see them as significant. Symbols are part of our world and in order for them to come alive, they require our participation. This represented a radical departure from a pre-modern, almost *magical* view of symbols to a modern *phenomenological* view of symbols, that is, from speculation about what is happening behind the scenes (who is pulling the strings?) to examining things as they are or as they appear in everyday life. There is no magic here. There is no intervention from *above* or *without* (extrinsic). Moreover, symbols have the potential to bring to the surface the presence of God from *within* (intrinsic). So, with Tillich and Rahner, symbols function like a catalyst in chemistry. A catalyst has the capacity to trigger or elicit a chemical reaction without itself undergoing change. For example, with the

Eucharist, rather than focusing on the words, actions and intentions of the priest in isolation from the faith community, the emphasis is on the shared experience of the faith community that values the symbols of bread and wine. The bread and wine as shared symbols evoke, from within the lives of the faithful, a sacramental experience of the presence of God. So, while the catalyst analogy does not prove anything, it helps to illustrate the dynamic associated with the nature of symbolism.

Now, here is the crux. Tillich's and Rahner's understanding of symbol plays a central role in their interpretation of the death-resurrection event, where the resurrection of Jesus is not lightning and thunder intervention or the resuscitation of a body.

On the contrary, resurrection is conceived in and grows out of the corporate experience of early faith communities. This means that the key to understanding the resurrection is intersubjectivity, where intersubjectivity recognizes that human identity, ideas and values are shaped by social interaction (recall the service for Jimi Hendrix).

While Tillich and Rahner do not expressly use the term *intersubjectivity*, it is implicitly present in the way they describe the dynamic of the resurrection, unfolding within the faith experience of the disciples. Further, their use of symbol, with its emphasis on experience and the notion of God as present in, or intrinsic to, experience is plausible. It makes sense of how we see our world. Furthermore, it helps explain the importance of the Christ figure over and above the Jesus of history. The historical Jesus, no matter how good the reconstruction, is still a reconstruction.

While historical reconstruction has a place in Tillich and Rahner, the emphasis is on the contemporary meaning of Christ. The contemporary meaning is discovered by means of our experience and part of that discovery can be explained in terms of the dynamic of symbol. In this context, the historical Jesus is the tangible aspect of the Christ symbol, which in the past triggered new theological insights and experiences from within the life of the early disciples. However, it is the contemporary experience of Christ *the symbol of God* that brings life in the present. Therefore, a symbolic interpretation does not mean that something is less than real or non-factual. On the contrary, a symbolic interpretation is a potent twenty-first century way of looking at and living in the world.

In the Flesh

In this chapter, the focus is on the death and resurrection of Jesus. The shorthand term for this is *the death-resurrection event*, and this is partly the case because Tillich and Rahner saw the death and the resurrection as two sides of the one coin. Further, for them, the Incarnation is integrally related to the death-resurrection event.

In preparation for the discussion of the death-resurrection event, I need to make some general remarks about the Incarnation. In short, the Incarnation is a classic symbol of presence. Traditionally, the Incarnation is about the transcendent God coming into the world in human form (John 1). In the popular mind, the focus is on the birth of the Christ-child (Matthew 1-2, Luke 1-2). However, the idea of the Incarnation loses credibility if the focus is *solely* on the birth stories. For a start, there are a number of biological and literary problems here. First, if we interpret the birth stories in Matthew and Luke *actually/factually*, all sorts of problems materialize. For instance, a virgin birth is not possible on the basis of our biological understanding of human birth. Second, the birth stories are not found in the Gospels of Mark and John. They are only in Matthew and Luke. How important or well known were these stories in the first place, if two of the Gospels do not include them? If they knew the stories, why would they choose to leave them out? Third, the differences between Matthew's and Luke's stories are significant and cannot easily be dismissed or reconciled. That is, if we compare these stories *literally* all sorts of problems emerge, which reinforce the critical judgment that they are more theology than history. Fourth, stories are important bearers of wisdom (existential insights). In the present case, the point of these stories is not that "God broke the rules of modern biology with the birth of this baby" but "new wisdom has come into this world in the adult life of Jesus" and this has been retrospectively celebrated and memorialized in the stories of his birth.

In this view, the Christ-child is a symbol of a new understanding, where God is not distant and unmoved, but intimately involved in human existence. Decisively, this God is vulnerable and enters into human suffering. This God is present. Nonetheless, this God was understood primarily in theistic terms, which meant the early Church spent the next 400 years trying to explain how a *universal* God could be involved in the world, in a *particular* life, and remain transcendent (holy or distinct).

With this in mind, it is time to look at Tillich's and Rahner's understanding of the Incarnation. It will soon become apparent that they do not concentrate their energies on the birth stories, but on the theological problem of acknowledging and affirming the presence of God in the world.

Two points will be made concerning the significance of the Incarnation in Tillich and Rahner. First, for Tillich and Rahner, while the Incarnation is the decisive expression of presence, absence is also part of the experience of the Incarnation.

With Tillich, absence has an explicit role in his theology of the Incarnation. It means Jesus, the definitive expression of presence, experiences the absence of God because he participates in the estrangement of human existence. Jesus himself encounters and contends with the problems, vagaries and delights of life. With Rahner, absence has an implicit role in his theology of the Incarnation, which becomes more explicit in conjunction with the death-resurrection event. For him, it is critical that Jesus the Christ was fully human, "He has a true body capable (before his resurrection) of suffering", that is, prior to the resurrection, Jesus was capable of experiencing suffering. This means that, if Christ was fully human, then he had the capacity to experience suffering and this includes the experience of absence. After all, absence is the *universal* experience of the hiddenness of God in *human* history.

Second, in the face of modernity, the Incarnation in Tillich and Rahner is a vigorous affirmation of the presence of God in the world. However, their claim that God is *uniquely present* in the Incarnation does not resonate with our current appreciation of religious pluralism and various philosophical concerns. They themselves knew that there was a tension here between, on the one hand, their conviction that the Incarnation was *the* decisive expression of presence and on the other hand, their respect for other religions. Ironically, their attempts to create a theology that accounts for other religions submerged the very tension they tried to resolve.

Toward the end of his career, Tillich was not fully comfortable with his own position on world religions, such that he expressed a desire to re-visit his theology and modify his view. Even so, it seems that the *absolute* uniqueness of Christ was still the basis of his Christian master-narrative, or at the least it functioned implicitly as the ultimate measure of the comparative value of other religions. All this betrays complex and unsolved problems. For example, how can a universal and transcendent God be found in a particular person, time and place? For Tillich and Rahner, this problem is a corollary of their metaphysical speculation.

In summary, for Tillich and Rahner, the meaning of the Incarnation is about the presence of God in the world, which is manifest in the life of Jesus. This implies that Jesus experienced the absence of God, because he was *fully* human. Nonetheless, they do not overcome the problem of trying to reconcile their understanding of Christ and Christianity with their desire to respect the validity of other religions, mainly because they worked on the basis that they, at least implicitly, had *the* master-narrative.

Redescribing the Death-Resurrection Event

To reiterate, the older I get, the more I am attracted to following Jesus. As the leading player in an emancipation movement of women and men, he exemplifies and expresses something of presence. In the name of love, he challenges the religious, social and political barriers of his day, in order to incorporate marginalized people into a community of grace. Therefore, I hope this book will help Jesus find a place at your next dinner party. While he would ask you challenging questions about social justice and inclusion, he would enjoy the wine, the food and above all, your company.

However, to have a fresh look at Jesus, a few things have to be explored. This is why it was important to establish earlier that a twenty-first century God is not found in the sky but in the web of relationships. All this has implications for the Jesus question, as it allows us to reclaim the significance of the death-resurrection event in relation to the life and experience of the faith community (without resorting to a divine-puppeteer). But there are other obstacles that get in the way of a full and fresh appreciation of Jesus. Expressly, an actual/factual interpretation of the resurrection of Jesus is troublesome. So let me say something about the problems associated with the resurrection in general and the problems surrounding the use of the word *body*.

To begin, the issue at stake here is the nature of the description of the resurrection. That is, while I accept the resurrection as one of the mysteries of faith, this does not mean we cannot think about how we reinterpret it for our era. In fact, there are many ways of describing the resurrection. Let me canvass some of the major issues associated with such a description.

First, the idea of a *bodily* resurrection poses problems ranging from lack of strong evidence to the modern understanding of how events are *caused* in the world. More so, the resurrection as the *resuscitation* of a *physical* body is fraught with problems, in terms of what we know about the natural world, as well as the deficit of corroborating evidence. Further, arguments for a *physical* body frequently hinge on the idea of the empty tomb. The empty tomb has iconic status in Christian piety. It is as though the mere utterance of the phrase "the empty tomb" ends all arguments. Sentiment aside, it is weak evidence in that it does not necessarily prove anything. Moreover, it presumes we can rely on the biblical stories as reliable historical accounts. But these accounts are more theological reflections than historical descriptions. Furthermore, the idea of a *bodily* resurrection is partly driven by the need to defend a version of theism. Once again, the presumed inerrancy of the Bible leads to circular reasoning. That is, God can intervene and raise Jesus from the dead, body and all, and we know this is true because the resurrection stories depict God's successful intervention.

Second, there are problems with an alternative argument that claims that the resurrection of Jesus involves *a spiritual body*. The argument goes like this: we know God cannot intervene and break the laws of nature, but the resurrection of Jesus is a special case because it's a special kind of body, namely, a *spiritual* body. In horse racing parlance, this is *an each way bet* and it is typical of the theological and logical quandaries defenders of soft theism find themselves in. Besides, the term *spiritual body* in popular usage is an oxymoron. That is, we do not normally describe a body as being spiritual, unless we mean the body is not material or it is not real (but ghostly). Of course, the counter argument can be made that, when we use the word *body* in the phrase *a spiritual body*, we are using it metaphorically or symbolically. The inference is that it is not a material body. If it is not a material body, is it real?

Third, the term *body* in the West carries with it enormous historical, cultural and religious baggage, such that, when we use *body* in everyday speech, we normally mean a *material* body.

Now, the idea of a material body is steeped in the Enlightenment's split between matter and spirit. Certainly, I question the grounds of this rigid dualism. Nevertheless, in trying to retain the term *body*, exponents of *a spiritual body* are fighting a challenging credibility battle. For the more we try and argue that a spiritual body is not like a material body, the more difficult it becomes to use the term *body* in the first place (and the more we capitulate to modernity's master-narrative that the material is separate from and superior to the spiritual). Further, I suspect that the motivation for wanting to retain the word *body*, at all costs, has to do with the issue of credibility. This is because, in everyday speech, a body is real, actual or factual, because it is material. Hence, the reluctance to drop the term *body*, because *no body* is equated with *not real*, that is if the resurrection did not involve a body of sorts, then it did not happen. But something happened.

I would argue that, just as we say our thoughts, memories and feelings are real, although they are not material, the ambiguous experience of the disciples, which is intangible, is no less real. It can also be argued that, on the basis of my redescription, the death-resurrection event can be affirmed where the corporate experience of the early faith communities, in which the resurrection of Jesus is conceived, is the *tangible* body of Christ-in-the-world. This redescription transfers attention away from the early Church's opaque formulations, which focus on what happened to the individual Jesus (and walk into modernity's *material/spiritual* snare), to the postmodern's appreciation of experience, especially shared experience.

Moreover, the concept of shared experience honors the life of Christian communities and is consonant with the emphasis on the faith community in the Gospels and letters of the Apostle Paul. In summary, some traditional descriptions of the resurrection, which have a legitimate place in the prayers and liturgies of the Church, can be obstacles to taking a fresh look at Jesus, because they were developed in a very different time and place to our twenty-first century Western world.

So, let's interpret Tillich's and Rahner's views of the death-resurrection event through the lens of the ambiguity of experience as absence and presence. For Tillich, the death of Jesus is the definitive expression of the absence of God, because it is the decisive experience of estrangement. That is, Jesus experienced absence. This is part and parcel of what it means to say that Jesus lived a normal/human life in the real world. So, in his death, which is the definitive experience of suffering, Jesus experienced the absence of God. Further, the traditional words uttered by Jesus from the Cross, in the Gospels of Mark and Matthew, eloquently capture the pain of the silence of God "My God, my God, why have you forsaken me?" Jesus knew the anguish of desertion. Furthermore, in Tillich the absence of God constitutes an experience of a vacuum rather than the *actual* absence of God. Thus, on the one hand, even when we do not experience God, God is present, because our unity with God cannot be destroyed. On the other hand, when we do not experience God, we feel the void and the conviction that only God can fill the void.

The importance of absence is evident in Tillich's discussions on estrangement. For him, estrangement means we lose ourselves and our sense of place. It is a painful reminder of our human limitations. To be human, is to live on the edge, that is, this experience is an encounter with the abyss. Nonetheless, the experience of absence can be a precursor to an experience of presence; "The God above God of theism is present, although hidden, in every divine-human encounter". For Tillich, this is a mystery which has been hidden.

The paradox of religion is that in and through Jesus, the symbol of God, this mystery has now been revealed. Lastly, the importance of absence in Tillich is illustrated by his understanding of atonement, where atonement concerns the role the death of Jesus played in bringing about reconciliation between God and humankind. In Tillich, the doctrine of atonement has a secondary role in his theology, because in the face of absence, reconciliation has been taking place in and through the life of

Jesus, as his life has mediated the healing effects of the presence of God.

Tillich claims the resurrected Jesus has "the character of spiritual presence". He links this presence with *the experience of the disciples*. Significantly, it is this link with the experience of the disciples that makes it possible for us to talk about the symbol of resurrection in our era, without the aid of his speculative trappings.

Certainly, Tillich acknowledges that his reflections on the resurrection are highly *theoretical*. Nonetheless, he asserts that a *real* experience lies behind the resurrection stories, in spite of their theological embellishments. Consequently, the disciples adopted the Jewish symbol of resurrection because it was commensurate with their experience of presence. That is, an old and familiar symbol of resurrection made sense of their new experience of presence. For Tillich, the disciples' experience of presence, and their naming of this experience as resurrection, is an integral part of the resurrection. They are one with the reality of the resurrection. Thus, the resurrection is conceived in the experience of the disciples.

Tillich recognizes that there is a danger here of reducing the resurrection to merely psychological explanation. Consequently, it is important for him to clarify the nature of the relationship between the meaning of presence and the role of the disciples. His clarification has two elements: the resurrection is not an *ordinary* experience of presence and the event is also made up of the fact of the resurrection and *their reception* of the resurrection. First of all, the disciples' resurrection experience of presence is an *extraordinary* experience, because the resurrected Jesus inaugurates a new reality in and through their mutual experience. However, this cannot be tested in a scientific (or objective) sense, since it can only be received as a gift of grace, expressed in and through human experience. Second, the disciples themselves are the all-important "history-bearing" group; they are not bit players or movie extras in the divine drama as a new chapter in history has been *written in* their experience.

The main problem is the status of this event. Is it history? Certainly, that the disciple's experience *something* is historical, and that something is the reality of the resurrection.

In summary, Tillich has been criticized for presenting a modern, individualistic picture of humankind. His version of human existence is abstract and impersonal. Nonetheless, his linking of resurrection and the disciples' experience (their *reception*) prefigures something of our era's understanding of the role of intersubjectivity, which acknowledges that human identity, ideas and values are shaped appreciably by social inter-action as well as biological and environmental factors. Subsequently, the resurrection is conceived by Tillich as occurring within the mutual experience of the faith community of early disciples. Therefore, the resurrection of Jesus is not lightning and thunder intervention but rather it is something which is conceived in, and grows out of, the corporate experience of early faith communities. This experience, in community, is the body of Christ in the world.

However, while we can leave to one side something of Tillich's metaphysical speculation; it is hard to overcome some of the inherent problems associated with his version of soft theism. The stumbling block is his two-fold claim that the presence of God is the *human awareness of its participation in Divine life* but *God is not part of the world*. Tillich describes this contradiction as a paradox and argues that paradoxes are a natural and inevitable part of human existence. But this is not a convincing explanation.

For Rahner, the significance of the death of Jesus needs to be seen in the light of his view of the Incarnation. The presence of God in the life of Jesus represents God's promise, God's tangible commitment to humankind and the world. The death of Jesus represents the fulfillment of that promise. Moreover, the meaning of the promise is not found in the idea of placating a remote and wrathful God, but rather it is disclosed in Jesus' choice to honor what was taking place in and through his own life in the world. In other words, his death was the logical outcome of his commitment to the way of God. Rahner's view of the death of Jesus is also influenced by his view of our inherent human limitations.

We accept the inevitability of death, which is our ultimate limitation, and we claim and honor the gift of life. In this instance, the death of Jesus is a true measure of the value of the divine gift, in that God, rather than demanding satisfaction, yearns for our transformation. Further, while Jesus was influenced by an emancipatory movement from Galilee, his life and example in turn shaped and inspired that movement, that faith community, which became the ground of the resurrection. Rahner describes this transformation of humanity in terms of symbols. Thus, the cross is a symbol which effects/changes something in and through the faith community. But what about the resurrection?

Rahner's theology of the resurrection can be understood in two ways. In negative terms, he asserts that there is a unity of spirit and body and this unity undergoes the same fate. This means that the resurrection is not a revival of the spirit of Jesus or the resuscitation of his body or an extrinsic event. In positive terms, resurrection means the abiding validity of the person of Jesus. Jesus has been vindicated as savior and the full reality of the presence of God in him has been mediated to the world. But Rahner, by his own admission, can only provide informed *clues* about the nature of this abiding validity, because resurrected existence is a different mode of existence. Now this looks like another version of a *spiritual* body. This perception, however, is countered by Rahner's understanding of human nature, which is the backdrop for appreciating the death-resurrection event, that is, the resurrection is premised on our innate capacity for openness toward God. Moreover, the experience of the early disciples demonstrates the significance of this innate openness. Specifically, the resurrection experience of the disciples gives them retrospectively new knowledge about Jesus. With the wisdom of hindsight, they now know the spiritual significance of the earthly Jesus. This is the theological and explanatory power of the appearance accounts (stories about the appearance of the *risen* Jesus). Using mythological language and motifs, these stories depict the birth of resurrection-faith in the life of the early Church; "Jesus is risen into the faith of the disciples".

Like Tillich, there is more than a hint of postmodern intersubjectivity in Rahner's interpretation of the death-resurrection event, since the experience of the disciples is a constitutive part of the resurrection. Nevertheless, Rahner is aware of the limits of his argument. He acknowledges the non-historical character of the resurrection, but insists that something *real* lies behind the appearance stories. They point to "the experience that Jesus is alive". Hence, in spite of its speculative style, Rahner's interpretation of the appearance stories is persuasive. In this context, the appearance stories play an important symbolic role, because they evoke faith in the resurrection and by doing this they also bear witness to the continuing validity of Jesus for later generations. Thus, the appearance stories are literary catalysts or symbols, which inspire and articulate the faith of the Church. So, let me summarize the contributions of our two shepherds.

For Tillich, the death-resurrection consists of two interdependent symbols. The cross is the symbol that expresses Christ's participation in existence and the resurrection is the symbol that expresses Christ's transcendence of the limits of existence. However, there is an unresolved tension in his work between: the gap between God and the world *and* his claim that the resurrection overcomes the gap. In the end, I am not convinced that the problem as defined by Tillich has been overcome, whereas Rahner's anthropology, with God working from *the inside out*, fares better. In this setting, the symbol of the cross is an invitation to embrace absence as the beginning of a process of transformation, where the resurrection is the culmination of the process.

Significantly, the resurrection is realized in the disciples' experience as presence. In sum, by using the idea of the ambiguity of experience as presence and absence, Tillich and Rahner provide useful insights into our understanding of Jesus, particularly his death and resurrection. However, they were writing for a different era. As a result, they use a speculative style of argument (with a slightly sanctimonious air), in trying to explain and justify the significance of Jesus, which does not ring true with our era's style and concerns.

In conclusion, there are differences between Tillich and Rahner but there are similarities too. In terms of personal biography, they are different people from different religious traditions, using different methods. In particular, their interpretation of the nature of human existence is the main source of difference.

In Tillich, there is an underlying mood of pessimism regarding human nature. His view of humankind has something of what has been described as "a fixed nature". It is no coincidence that Tillich places much weight on the symbol of The Fall (the story of Adam and Eve in Genesis 2-3 the second creation story). In Rahner, there is a pervasive optimism about humankind living in and by the grace of God. Further, the way Tillich and Rahner interpret absence is an important instance of the differences between the two theologians. Absence is basic to their respective understandings of experience, but there are subtle variations.

Where Tillich's interpretation of absence is governed largely by his understanding of the fragmented nature of human existence, Rahner's interpretation is governed largely by his understanding of God as experienced by humankind, which has an inbuilt orientation toward God. Furthermore, Tillich's concept of absence is a comparatively static quality (as in "God's vacuum"). For him, humankind is burdened with absence because of the withdrawal of God. As a symptom of estrangement, absence is something to be stoically endured.

In contrast, Rahner's concept of absence is a comparatively

dynamic quality of God (as in "God's hiddenness"). Humankind is faced with the experience of absence, because this is the nature of God, but it is also a source of mystery. The critical issue here is what can we learn from our German shepherds about experience and the significance of common or mutual experience?

I am trying to identify ingredients for a twenty-first century understanding of faith. This entails an acknowledgement of a striking ambivalence in our era toward religion. This also involves acknowledging the reality of suffering and the problem of the silence of God, which in turn forces us to rethink and redescribe God in terms of absence as well as presence. Okay, so what does this have to say in specific terms about the Christian faith? Well, Christianity rises or falls on the basis of its claims about Jesus. There is no avoiding this. However, by taking up the Jesus question and looking at it from the perspective of presence and absence, important grounds are established for a relevant and credible Jesus.

The lynch pin in all this surrounds the death-resurrection event. With the aid of our two German shepherds, we have re-visited the death-resurrection event. In relation to the resurrection, the key insight has to do with the postmodern term *intersubjectivity*. In Tillich and Rahner, the resurrection takes place in the shared (intersubjective) experience of the early faith communities. This insight simultaneously downgrades the opaque and questionable aspects of pre-modern Jesus stories and dogma and upgrades and reinforces the importance of the faith-community.

This is because a transforming experience of presence takes place in community, which gives rise to a new insight into the significance of the life and death of Jesus. This insight does not rely on an external God interfering in human events. There is no lightning and thunder. The world is in God and God is in the world. Nor does it rely on magical or quasi-magical interpretations. On the contrary, the notions of community and symbol and the importance of human perceptions in symbolic actions are all understandable and accessible. Moreover, I do not claim that this view of God, Jesus and the death-resurrection is demonstrable or that it can be explained completely in rational terms. But it is plausible.

Finally, the resurrection does not stand alone. If it is the quintessential expression of presence, then the crucifixion is the quintessential expression of absence. In traditional religious language, the act of grace and the experience of suffering are one. They are symptomatic of the poignancy of the presence and absence of God in the world. Therefore, the symbol of the resurrection speaks today because it is not removed from the experience of absence, but rather it finds its ground in the silence of God. It is only in the cross that our *small deaths* are acknowledged.

In the cross, the figure of Jesus experiences the definitive experience of absence. In the resurrection, the presence of God is manifested in the life of the faith community.

Excursion, Sign and Symbol: In Tillich and Rahner, symbols are inherently ambiguous. This is because the significance of a symbol is dependent upon the perception (experience) of an individual or a group that attributes significance to the symbol. However, Tillich makes a special case for a *symbol* over a *sign*. For him, while signs and symbols both point beyond themselves, only "the symbol participates in the reality which is symbolized". But is this simply a theological sleight of hand? Tillich's distinction is very fuzzy. Moreover, Rahner acknowledges that this type of distinction is problematic. Therefore, I take the position that the distinction between symbols and signs is relative and based largely on the fact that an individual or a group *attributes to a sign* the privileged status of symbol. For instance, the Eucharist or Holy Communion is a meaningful symbol for many Christians, but it is arguably a mundane or a meaningless sign for Quakers (The Society of Friends) and members of the Salvation Army. In terms of the resurrection, the concept of symbol plays a vital role. In general, Jesus of Nazareth is the symbol of God. In particular, some of the disciples discover after the crucifixion, in the known symbol of the resurrection, a way of understanding their new life-transforming and shared experience of the presence of God in the world.

CHAPTER 6

SHEER PRESENCE

I see a compelling need for an understanding of God, Jesus and the Church, which incorporates absence. By doing this, we lay claim to a new understanding of presence in which presence though passing is profoundly humanizing. And this is where faith comes into it. By faith, I do not mean learning by rote large chunks of the Bible or reciting parrot-fashion a list of properly vetted and authorized doctrines. Faith is an orientation to life that gives us the wisdom to live as best we can with the reality of absence; it also makes the apprehension and enjoyment of presence possible. Faith is an attitude, which engages with the world, incorporates doubt and is expressed in concert with others.

Faith as Engagement

It is time to present an impressionist painting of a faith fit for the twenty-first century. It is impressionistic because of the ambiguous nature of experience, the complexity of life and the mystery of God. It involves reinterpreting the meaning of God and finding a place for Jesus that will not embarrass our dinner guests. It is about promoting the stuff of good religion, which builds lives and creates community and recognizes the value of our mutual and collective experience of God in the world. In this setting, faith is a process of engagement with the world and God. *Engagement with the world* means faith cannot retreat from the big issues of the day and the biggest issue is the question of suffering. *Engagement with God* means that the big issues, especially suffering, force us to rethink and redescribe God because *the old man in the sky* has let us down.

The process of engagement is a life-long enterprise, because both the ambiguity of life and the mystery of God mean that we never arrive at *the* answer. In fact, the Grand Tour, yes the journey, is the thing. Moving on, letting go and discovering, that's the nature of faith and it requires an attitude of passionate engagement. Along the way, we will discover new wisdom for the journey, which will inspire and sustain us.

A twenty-first century faith has a normal, everyday look about it. Let me explain. I was recently in Borders book shop in San Francisco, next to Bloomingdales. I had just purchased the mandatory swag of holiday reading books. As I was savoring my acquisitions, I noticed at the next table a middle aged man making origami animals from dollar bills. This seemed a natural thing. There was no fuss or clamor in the bookstore, as he quietly made successive paper animals while gently sipping his coffee, but there was a palpable sense of shared community and mutual goodwill. One by one, staff members came from all over the store and greeted him warmly and he responded with equal affection. Only a few words were exchanged. The warmth, the manner of greeting and the respectful space between the words and actions, evoked a sense of presence. Okay, there is always the possibility that I was the only one in the store who felt inspired. But I could not help feel a kind of reverence, even awe, in this shared experience. While this was not an explicitly religious gathering, it was sacramental and it served as a reminder that the Church does not, and cannot, own presence. It also reminds us that an encounter with presence is an exquisite moment, soon gone. Filled and emptied, only a trace remains, yet we have been entrusted with a new memory of encounter (and the ancients knew something about the power of memory).

Where to now? Well, it is important to remind ourselves of where we began. We began with a wedding reception and Table 17, the miscellaneous table and the obvious discomfort of wedding guests at the presence of a member of the clergy. We began with the recognition that religion is a difficult and cantankerous creature. We recognized that a life-giving, life-grounding faith begins with the acknowledgement that religion is out of favor in the twenty-first century West.

There are two aspects to this acknowledgement. First Christianity, along with the Church, the Bible, God and Jesus, is cause for general embarrassment. Second, God is a problem because God is absent in the experience of suffering. Consequently, the experience of absence forces us to rethink God. I have not attempted to establish a proof of God's existence. I have assumed that there are many ways of seeing or understanding God and I have asserted that new descriptions of God can enrich human life and community by embracing the idea of absence. So, if there is a God, then God is not a pre-modern old man in the sky. If there is a God, then God has to speak to the twenty-first century. If there is a God, then God cannot be turned into a commodity. In this context, faith is about engagement, it is a feisty existential attitude, a life-journey, which takes place in and through the ambiguity of experience. Above all, it accepts the contingent nature of existence and incorporates doubt.

Faith and Doubt

In the heart of darkness, there were many occasions when a London cabbie saved us from a fate worse than death. London traffic is torrid, especially in the suitably named *congestion zone*. There is not a straight road in sight and millions of dead-ends. We often got lost, despite having the latest tourist maps. Sometimes we would rationalize the whole exercise with "Oh well, it's a beautiful day in a great city" but after two hours we would turn to the omnipresent London cabbie for assistance. The London cabbies are a remarkable group of people. Maybe we were just lucky, but all the cabbies we met were helpful, cheery and knew where they were going. In contrast, one rainy evening in Sydney,

I was catching a taxi to the Town Hall. The driver had no idea of its whereabouts. I do not think he even knew what I meant by "Town Hall" (even though, we were only two miles away from our destination). In Hong Kong, the taxi drivers knew where they were going, but it is a heck of a drive getting there at speed, in their ancient red Toyota Crowns. In Bermuda, the taxi driver plays a vital social role. Like many Bermudians, they beep their horns not as a warning, but as a salutation to friends and strangers alike. In New York, it's something out of Wagner, as cab drivers move frenetically against threatening but invisible forces. They are courteous to passengers but, in relation to the other cars, they take no prisoners. The New York cabbie uses the car horn like an axe, cutting the air in a vain attempt to clear the log-jam, especially if they have to wait more than twenty seconds. In San Francisco, we stuck with the cable cars. Be that as it may, life is a congestion zone, characterized by ambiguity and doubt. But like the ubiquitous and transient London cabbie, there is presence. Delicate and evanescent, an experience nonetheless that is capable of transforming us.

A twenty-first century faith demands that: we acknowledge the reality of suffering, we question unqualified commitment to theism, especially hard theism, and we relinquish remnants of the Church's historic commitment to idealizing life, faith and families (remember Mother's Day). Let us name the silence of God. Further, I suspect that the awareness of *the absent God* starts early in life and, when it emerges, it is a coming of age. Yes, it is a loss of innocence, the end of a dream, as well as the beginning of wisdom. So, while I have a passionate faith in God, it is a very different kind of God from the Sunday school God of my childhood.

In spite of all these changes, however, the question of truth is central. A twenty-first century faith, however, demands that we relinquish the idea that the Church has exclusive possession of truth. On this note, it is worth revisiting the comparison between the fundamentalist and mainstream types of Christianity. The terms fundamentalist and mainstream Christianity represent an important pair of concepts. The purpose of the pair is to clarify key issues. This is not to say that either concept represents a monochrome entity. In the mainstream Church, there is a great deal of variety among mainstream Anglican, Catholic, Orthodox and Protestant churches. Within each of these traditions, there is a variety of beliefs and practices ranging from traditional to liberal, and while Christian fundamentalism is primarily a reformed Protestant phenomenon; it is now prevalent in quarters of Anglicanism (for instance, the Diocese of Sydney, Australia). As a comparison, traditionalism in the Catholic Church comes close to fundamentalism. Traditionalism, like fundamentalism, is in part a reaction to the impact of modernity (Darwinism, theories of evolution). However, fundamentalism is oriented primarily toward a text (Bible, Koran), whereas traditionalism is oriented primarily toward Church authority, structure and tradition as embodied by the figure of the Pope.

Fundamentalism and mainstream Christianities represent types, and the contrast between the two leads to a greater under-standing of the complex nature of Christianity. The foremost difference concerns the issue of truth. Consequently, I have criti-cized fundamentalism on the basis of its absolutist attitude toward the issue of truth. The idea that an individual or a group has sole possession of *the* truth is incredible. By the same token, this does not mean that there is no place for truth in an alternative understanding of Christianity. If we are going to talk meaning-fully about the big life issues, then we have to be able to talk about truth at some level. The real danger is what happens to us if we learn to live with uncertainty and relinquish our claims to the exclusive ownership of truth? Do we fall into the abyss? Well, yes we do, but the abyss is the crucible of faith. In the face of absence, we also run the risk of experiencing presence. So, by relinquishing our tight hold on truth, we make it possible to discern and articulate a faith that is fit for the twenty-first century.

Faith is messy, heart-pumping, life-giving stuff, because it involves wrestling with the big questions. We do not solve the questions, but we discover hope in the questioning. This means that we do not take any question lying down, and if we do, we get up and start again. This means that we do not take up this challenge as lone isolated hero figures, but in community with others, who have also taken themselves on. We also take on God, because a twenty-first century God does not need to be excused or protected or defended but engaged, for it's in the process of engagement that we discover new experiences and dimensions of grace.

I am appealing to people who want to explore faith and make the journey, where faith is a life-long adventure. Faith involves engagement with God and the world, accepting doubt and recognizing the complexity of existence. Implicitly, faith entails a kind of humility. Now clearly the word *humility* is loaded, but I do not mean anything like appeasing, cringing or groveling. No, it is not the feigned humility of Charles Dickens's Uriah Heep. By humility, I am thinking about being grounded. The word *humility* comes from *humus*, which is a life-producing ingredient in soil. Being grounded is conducive to the development of an adult faith. This kind of faith is discovered by being open to the world and not by defending a biblical text, a moral edict, a dogmatic position, or a venerable institution. Faith, as a way of engagement, means that I am not abandoning God. On the contrary, I am passionately seeking a robust yet fruitful description of God, which is fit for our time. This type of faith also includes a place for intellectual rigor, because a faith which accepts doubt and lives with contingency must harness all possible resources, intellectual and otherwise, to ensure that it is trustworthy and life-enhancing. It involves letting go of long-held, and deeply cherished, images and convictions that have served us well, but have lost their spiritual, ethical and existential potency. It is a small death, but it brings life.

In Concert with Others

In the twenty-first century, there is an intriguing ambivalence toward religion. For some, religion is becoming increasingly irrelevant. For others religion, in one form or another, is becoming more and more important. I am interested in the God problem, and while the God problem is bigger than the question of suffering, the question of suffering poses the greatest challenge to a contemporary description of God. Suffering is a reality and God is not in control. In the long run, however, it is no use blaming God. While there is a time and a place for railing at God, this is often a signal that it is time to move on from the view of God that simultaneously holds God personally responsible for suffering *and* absolves us of personal responsibility. Suffering happens! In some situations, we are directly and personally accountable for it, because of the things we did or failed to do (as in the case of genocide). In other cases, we are implicitly accountable because of our shared humanity (as in our response to disaster). Personal and corporate responsibility is an important issue on ethical grounds alone. However, there is more to it than that, because a twenty-first century understanding of God is found in the power of shared experience. Remember the Guarani. Captain Mendoza deserved to have his throat cut, but Guarani responded in grace, and in so doing, Mendoza encountered the presence of God in the world. Consequently, Mendoza had a new view of himself and the world. There was now a warts-and-all sense of self- acceptance, which enabled Mendoza to embrace his former enemies. While transitory, the salve of presence brings hope.

On that key note, let's revisit the major themes. I have taken a postmetaphysical approach to presence, in contrast to Neville and the glass of red wine. I am not trying to address the nature of God as my attention has been fixed on our experience of God. In particular, there is something important to be identified and explored in our ambiguous experience of God in the world. I have used some insights from our two German shepherds, without being captive to their era or their concerns. Implicit in the work of both Tillich and Rahner is the recognition that we need to allow a place for the experience of faith communities in the discernment of new wisdom. By limited, I do not mean that it is of negligible value, as the best theological insights continually emerge from the life of faith communities. I mean that other factors have to be considered (rational, historical, sociological factors). This is in contrast to fundamentalist communities, where the bible teacher or a particular community has the first and final say on the question of truth. Further, it is reasonable to presume that faith communities, as well as individual Christians, have helped to create, shape and sustain the Church's tradition and theology throughout history. The inference here is that the tradition and theology of the Church are both expressions and reflections of the corporate experience of faith communities. It is also reasonable to presume that, as gleaned from everyday speech, faith communities intuitively appreciate the importance of the concepts of experience, presence and absence. Faith communities know first hand the impact of absence and yearn for presence. It is no wonder then that the concepts of experience, presence and absence help shape and color, implicitly and explicitly, the spiritual and ecclesial life of faith communities. It is hard to imagine a discussion about the meaning of prayer, meditation, baptism or the Eucharist, which does not use the language of experience, presence and absence.

Consequently, the concept of the presence of God used here has not been *idealized*. In fact, the interplay of presence and absence honors the complexity and diversity of *real* human experience. Everyday people and faith communities experience ambiguity; that is, absence as well as presence, and the interplay between presence and absence says something about God in the world, God as experienced, perceived and interpreted.

In terms of implications, I am not convinced by traditional theism's approach to God and the world (as in the case of supernaturalism). By the same token, I am not willing to make easy concessions to secular accounts of the world that blithely separate the material from the spiritual. I presume that the nature of God and God's involvement in the world is complex and cannot be condensed neatly into theoretical models.

I am also critical of the wider society's habit of turning all manner of things into commodities (spirituality as a New Age hand bag) or its obsession with naive versions of truth and knowledge (the adoration of the fact). In all this, Jesus provides us with a clue. He is the touchstone for the discernment of new wisdom.

I am convinced of the relevance of the life and teachings of Jesus and the relevance of the emancipation movement that his name embodies. Nevertheless, it is important to show how first century aspects of the life of Jesus speak to the twenty-first century. The key example involves a reinterpretation of the death-resurrection event.

My interpretation of the ambiguity of experience as presence and absence grounds the death-resurrection event existentially and theologically. This is important for two reasons. First, a study of the significance of Jesus, that overemphasizes presence, runs the risk of failing to speak to faith communities who know the experience of absence. This is partly an argument for a relevant, humane and compassionate understanding of the significance of Jesus, but it is also an argument for the recognition of the public and social factors in discerning new wisdom. Thus, I earth the significance of Jesus in experience. Second, if experience has a role in the creation of new wisdom, then there is an inherent danger of the significance of Jesus becoming captive to a particular individual's or faith community's experience. However, experience alone is not privileged here over and above evidence and reason or coherence with other beliefs. My view of experience means that the study of the significance of Jesus is not captive to a particular faith community's experience. What is more, Tillich's and Rahner's interpretation of the death-resurrection event supports my argument.

For Tillich and Rahner, the resurrection of Jesus takes place in the life of the shared experience of the disciples. With Tillich, the death-resurrection event overcomes the limits of existence and the *fact* that God is not part of the world. In the process, the event promises humankind participation in divine life. Specifically, the cross is a symbol that expresses something of the depth of Jesus' experience of human existence, such that the cross is the definitive symbol of absence. For Rahner, the Incarnation means Christ experienced suffering and this includes the experience of absence. The symbol of the cross is therefore an invitation to the faithful to embrace absence as the inauguration of a transformative process that culminates in the resurrection. Further, Tillich and Rahner argue that the resurrection is realized in the disciples' experience as an experience of presence. For them, while presence is not material, something real lies behind the experience. However, they do not adequately define that *something real*. I am arguing that we ought to stay with experience, no matter how transient, and leave aside explicit metaphysical speculation. The central issue is that the experience of presence is conceived within the shared experience of the disciples (their intersubjective experience). The value of shared experience is that it builds community, where new wisdom is discerned through an encounter with presence, which in turn enriches and enhances the life of the faith community. It is not the case that presence is confined to the experience of a faith community, but rather the corporate experience of a faith community is conducive to encounters with the presence and absence of God and the creation of new wisdom. In other words, in order to encounter presence, it is not essential to be in tandem with others, but the apprehension and appreciation of presence is enhanced by a network of relationships that, like the Guarani, function as communities of grace.

At the Next Dinner Party

Here we have the source of Christianity's vitality. It is not ritual, dogma or neo-gothic wonders. It is grace. In the midst of absence, there is a transient yet humanizing expression of presence, which is experienced as grace.

We see it in the parable of the lost son (Luke 15:11-32). It is spelled out in the healing on the Sabbath (Mark 3:1-5).[168] The point of these ancient stories is not that "God has broken the laws of nature" but "new wisdom has come into the world" and this has been retrospectively celebrated and memorialized in the great symbols of the Church. So, why bother with Jesus? We bother with Jesus because he is a potent and impassioned symbol of grace. He is a life-affirming expression of the presence of God in the world. In the real world we are embroiled in the anguish of the human predicament, with all its disasters and delights, failures and successes. By naming and relegating the old man in the sky to the back blocks of history, the significance of the meaning of presence as embodied by Jesus and his community of equals becomes clearer. Yes, there is presence, which is always in the company of absence. Sweet presence, while fleeting, is life-renewing and memory making. Whether it's in a pub in Manhattan, a cab in London, or a bookstore in San Francisco, presence is encountered in many ways and consists of many layers of meaning. We cannot go back in time to capture and domesticate experiences of presence, but the experience has changed us and such encounters are celebrated with friends-in-community long after the event. With music, words, symbols and rituals we remember and relive the memory of encounters with presence.

Indeed, because of the importance of the shared nature of

experience (*inter*-subjective), a faith community is a natural habitat for the experience, remembrance and celebration of presence. However, this raises the curly problem of institutions, as institutions have a habit of spoiling the experience and diminishing community.

The Church, as institution, can get in the way of faith. Ironically, the experience of the absence of God can keep the Church honest. To reiterate, I am more interested in *exploring our experience* of God than *defining the nature* of God. But this does not mean that we cannot assert positive things about God. No, my reserve concerns the extent to which we can affirm precisely something about the mystery of God and the complexity of human experience.

Nevertheless, the central issue is that our theologies need to consider the absence of God we encounter in suffering. As we openly address the issue of suffering, we are forced to look at old and new descriptions of God. Consequently, the experience of presence and absence forces us to rethink the Church as well as God. While we will persist in exploring various understandings of God, as the journey's the thing, we know instinctively that God is *above* the God of theism and *beyond* the categories of theism and atheism.

The Church does not own God. We know intuitively that the Church, in order to be the Church, must continually aspire to cultivate religion without religion. An impossible task? Yes, but it is the prophetic vocation of the Church, as an institution living in the midst of absence and presence, to transcend its own investment in structures, privilege and power. In keeping with the Jesus tradition, the Church is an institution that is called to work faithfully toward deinstitutionalization. I am aware of many of the problems confronting the contemporary Church. The current division in the Anglican Communion over the issue of homosexuality is a case in point. In many ways, it is the result of the rise of and submission to the influence of fundamentalism.

Fundamentalism has hijacked the Anglican Church's agenda. In terms of the Anglican Church's history of tolerance, comprehensiveness and diversity, this is dangerous, as it is only a short leap from believing you possess the master-narrative to trying to *master* the lives of others. This is bad religion.

In the face of bad religion, there are days when I could easily drift out of the institution and into the world. But for goodness sake, it's my Church too. While we cannot avoid the cross-grained nature of institutions, because the seeds of institutions are sown wherever there are common interests and mutual experiences, we can ensure that our institutions are open and receptive to the destabilizing and life-renewing impact of the ambiguous experience of God. When the ambiguity of the experience is honored, we travel lightly and dare not attempt to play God.

This kind of theology is discovered in the web of evolving relationships (human, ecological, cosmological) and cultivated in the shared experience of faith communities. In concert with others, we simultaneously experience the sacred and discern new wisdom for twenty-first century living. In order to embrace this, we need to eschew: the myth of the perfect life, the Sunday school God, the meek and mild Jesus and the idea of Church as an unchanging institution. For most of us, with our ethical quandaries, quirky families, relationship issues, saturated lifestyles and innumerable commitments, life is lived in the congestion zone. Therefore, the ambiguity of experience is *the* starting point for a redescription of God and a renewed Church. It is also the starting point for a more inclusive global perspective, as we look beyond the horizon of the West to the global experience of suffering, that is, from our small deaths to the Holocaust, 9/11, Iraq, Afghanistan, Tibet, the Sudan and beyond.

So, what does life look like, if we respect the ambiguity of the experience of God? Well, there is presence, which keeps us alive and resilient. There is also absence, which keeps us earthed in real life and open to the world. And herein lays the genius of Jesus. I have chosen to follow the way of Jesus, because he was passionate about good religion. He unmasked and rejected bad religion. This friend of tax collectors and sinners loved a dinner party and set an example worth following. The meaning of his life impinges on me in solitude and through shared experiences. While such meaning is more than historical facts, it should not contradict historical or scientific insights. However, history and science cannot account for everything that makes human life worth living. While experience is slippery, there is new wisdom here that is discerned bit by bit, in faith-filled communities that are grounded in the incomprehensible mystery of God. This Jesus then, and the memory of his presence, is born again and again in the corporate experience of generations of faithful people, in spite of all the ecclesiastical tyrants and scoundrels.

While there are no perfect institutions, especially the Church, the ambiguity of presence and absence can keep the institution alive and life-giving.

The older I get, the more fascinated I am with the sayings and parables of Jesus and the charismatic figure that shines through them. Clearly, I am not talking about *the meek and mild Jesus* of Sunday school fame. While the name Jesus is cause for embarrassment at a dinner party, and that is not entirely a bad thing, I am convinced that an adult appreciation of Jesus serves as the decisive measure of the identity and purpose of the Church. Nevertheless, there is a lot of nonsense about Jesus, circulating in wider society and the Church, which prevents people from looking openly at the Jesus tradition. Much of the Jesus baggage has to do with our view of God. I have redescribed God and this has provided us with an opportunity to revisit the figure of Jesus. Undoubtedly, Jesus is central to the Christian tradition. He is Christianity's main ingredient and prevailing flavor. His life reveals the impact of presence in gracious actions of hospitality and inclusion that transcend religious, social and political barriers.

Ironically, the Church's collective memory of Jesus embodies an important prophetic critique of the pitfalls of institutions. This means that the figure of Jesus provides, through the cross and the resurrection experience of the disciples, a telling insight into the annihilating power of absence and the renewing power of presence.

Now here is the most delicious irony of all. The very Christianity, which is understandably out of favor with the latte-sipping, wine-quaffing, emailing West, has within its own living tradition something to offer. It is its experience of grace. Now the Church does not own grace, but in spite of itself, it has been open to and has celebrated life under grace for 2000 years. Certainly, we have not always honored this heritage, but the destabilizing effect of the ambiguity of the experience has continually unmasked our own hypocrisy and self-deception. Therefore, in order to stay real, healthy and open, the Church itself has to address constantly and courageously the question, "Why bother with Jesus?"

We bother with Jesus, because he reveals something primary about the character of grace. Unfortunately, the word *grace* seems bland, because it is often associated with being nice and respectable in a religious kind of way.

In the Jesus tradition, expressions of grace are counter-cultural. Today, a host of social and political factors largely determine whether we are *in* or *out*, *upstairs* or *downstairs* (and *don't forget your place*). In the Jesus tradition, we find our place. This means the Captain Mendozas of the world are welcomed back into the human community. In fact, this means we are all in.

Therefore, grace is not an ecclesiastical sedative but a disturbing expression of the presence of God, which recognizes our differences while transcending our divisions. This grace is not cheap or insipid; it is costly and revitalizing. It is found in the midst of an ambiguous life, with its small deaths and looming dangers. Nevertheless, as an expression of presence, grace cannot be distilled from the ether and bottled for human consumption. So while we met God in Bermuda, the experience of presence is always short-lived because presence, sweet presence, is sheer presence sitting precariously on the edge of the abyss. Soon gone, we learn to live without it, wisely making do, half expecting another unexpected encounter with the presence of God in the world.

FURTHER READING

Berger, P.L. *The Desecularization of the World: Resurgent Religion and World Politics*, (Grand Rapids, Michigan: Eerdmans, 1999).

Butler, C. *Postmodernism: A Very Short Introduction*, (Oxford: Oxford University Press, 2002).

Carr, E.H. *What is History?* (Hampshire: Palgrave, 1961, 1986, 2001); in this classic, Carr casts a keen eye over history-writing and the search for historical *facts*.

Caputo, J.D. *On Religion*, (London and New York: Routledge, 2001); written for popular consumption, it has insightful assessments of postmodern issues.

Everitt, N. and Fisher, A. *Modern Epistemology: A New Introduction*, (London: McGraw-Hill, 1995); a *readable* introduction to issues on truth and knowledge.

Moltmann, J. *God for a Secular Society*, (London: SCM Press, 1999).

O'Meara, T.F. *A Theologian's Journey*, (New York: Paulist Press, 2002); while this book is about O'Meara's *journey*, it is a good introduction to Karl Rahner.

Pauck, W. and Pauck, M. *Paul Tillich: His Life and Thought*, (San Francisco: Harper and Row, 1989).

Rorty, R. and Vattimo, G. *The Future of Religion*, S. Zabala ed., (New York: Columbia University Press, 2004, 2005); a little gem.

Ruthven, M. *Fundamentalism: The Search for Meaning*, (Oxford, New York: Oxford University Press, 2004); very useful.

Taylor, C. *A Secular Age*, (Cambridge, Massachusetts and London: Belknap Press, 2007).

Taylor, M.C. *After God*, (Chicago, London: University of Chicago Press, 2007).

If you would like to explore in depth the postmodern debate on God, and have the time, read M.C. Taylor's *After God* and Charles Taylor's *A Secular Age*. These works are not for the faint-hearted, but they are perceptive and rewarding.

Toulmin, S. *Cosmopolis: The Hidden Agenda of Modernity*, (Chicago: University of Chicago Press, 1990, 1992); a little dated, but Toulmin puts an original spin on modernity.

Other Books by Steven G. Ogden

The Presence of God in the World: A Contribution to Postmodern Christology based on the Theologies of Paul Tillich and Karl Rahner, (Bern, Berlin, Bruxelles, Frankfurt am Main, New York, Oxford, Wien: Peter Lang, 2007), an academic work, which may be helpful only for the intrepid reader.

BOOKS

O is a symbol of the world, of oneness and unity. In different cultures it also means the "eye," symbolizing knowledge and insight. We aim to publish books that are accessible, constructive and that challenge accepted opinion, both that of academia and the "moral majority."

Our books are available in all good English language bookstores worldwide. If you don't see the book on the shelves ask the bookstore to order it for you, quoting the ISBN number and title. Alternatively you can order online (all major online retail sites carry our titles) or contact the distributor in the relevant country, listed on the copyright page.

See our website **www.o-books.net** for a full list of over 500 titles, growing by 100 a year.

And tune in to myspiritradio.com for our book review radio show, hosted by June-Elleni Laine, where you can listen to the authors discussing their books.

mySpiritRadio